HIGHER ENGLISH
THE CRITICAL ESSAY

Mary M Firth
Andrew G Ralston

SCOTTISH
EXAMINATION
MATERIALS

HODDER
GIBSON

The Publishers would like to thank the following for permission to reproduce copyright material:
Photo credits Page 5 ©Donald Cooper/Photostage; Page 9 Columbia/Ronald Grant Archive; Page 15 20TH CENTURY FOX/Ronald Grant Archive; Page 17 COLUMBIA/THE KOBAL COLLECTION; Page 18 *The Changeling* by Robin Jenkins, by permission of Canongate; Page 21 Mary Evans Picture Library/Alamy; Page 32 *To Kill A Mockingbird* by Harper Lee, published by Vintage. Reprinted by permission of The Random House Group Ltd; Page 32 *Touching the Void* by Joe Simpson, published by Vintage. Reprinted by permission of The Random House Group Ltd; Page 40 UNIVERSAL/THE KOBAL COLLECTION; Page 42 PCL/Alamy; Page 51 UpperCut Images/Alamy; Page 61 Rob Bartee/Alamy; Page 67 Alan SCHEIN/Alamy; Page 75 Colin Palmer Photography/Alamy; Page 94 Clifford White/APL/PA Photos.
Acknowledgements Extracts from past exam papers are reprinted with the permission of the Scottish Qualifications Authority.

'Hands' from *Moortown Diary* by Ted Hughes is reproduced by permission of Faber and Faber Ltd; Extract from *After You've Gone*, Copyright © 2000 Maggie O'Farrell. Reproduced by permission of Headline Publishing Group Limited; 'Brooklyn Cop' from *The Poems of Norman MacCaig* by Norman MacCaig is reproduced by permission of Polygon, an imprint of Birlinn Ltd (www.birlinn.co.uk); The extract from 'Snake' by D H Lawrence is taken from *The Complete Poems of D H Lawrence*, published by the Wordsworth Poetry Library.

Every effort has been made to trace all copyright holders, but if any have been inadvertently overlooked the Publishers will be pleased to make the necessary arrangements at the first opportunity.

Although every effort has been made to ensure that website addresses are correct at time of going to press, Hodder Gibson cannot be held responsible for the content of any website mentioned in this book. It is sometimes possible to find a relocated web page by typing in the address of the home page for a website in the URL window of your browser.

Hachette's policy is to use papers that are natural, renewable and recyclable products and made from wood grown in sustainable forests. The logging and manufacturing processes are expected to conform to the environmental regulations of the country of origin.

Orders: please contact Bookpoint Ltd, 130 Milton Park, Abingdon, Oxon OX14 4SB. Telephone: (44) 01235 827720. Fax: (44) 01235 400454. Lines are open 9.00–5.00, Monday to Saturday, with a 24-hour message answering service. Visit our website at www.hoddereducation.co.uk. Hodder Gibson can be contacted direct on: Tel: 0141 848 1609; Fax: 0141 889 6315; email: hoddergibson@hodder.co.uk

© Mary M Firth and Andrew G Ralston 2008
First published in 2008 by
Hodder Gibson, an imprint of Hodder Education, an Hachette Livre UK Company,
2a Christie Street
Paisley PA1 1NB

ISBN-13: 978 0340 966 563

Impression number   5 4 3
Year   2012 2011 2010

Cover photo Paul Hart/iStockphoto.com
Illustrations by Moira Munro
Typeset in Adobe ITC Garamond 11pt by DC Graphic Design Limited, Swanley Village, Kent.
Printed in Great Britian by MPG Book Group, Bodmin.

A catalogue record for this title is available from the British Library

Contents

Introduction

It goes without saying that you are aiming for a pass in your Higher English critical essay paper. But how do you achieve the desired grade?

It is not enough just to know your texts well and to learn your notes thoroughly. There are also certain skills that you must acquire if you are to achieve the best possible mark. In addition, there are certain misguided practices that may prevent you getting more than an average mark, or may even cause you to fail. These can trap unwary candidates, even if they have studied carefully. Learning to avoid them is essential if you are to achieve top marks. Working through this book will help you master the skills and avoid the pitfalls!

However, skills can't be explained on their own: you must be able to put them into practice. A number of texts that are widely used in Higher English classes are referred to in the course of this book.

Drama (plays):
Romeo and Juliet by William Shakespeare
Macbeth by William Shakespeare

Prose (novels and short stories):
Lord of the Flies by William Golding
The Changeling by Robin Jenkins

Poetry:
'Snake' by DH Lawrence
'Brooklyn Cop' by Norman MacCaig

Don't worry if you haven't studied these texts. Explanations are given in such a way that prior knowledge is not needed.

The skills you acquire from working through the exercises can then be applied to other texts you have studied in school or at college. (Note that, although the Higher English paper also includes the option to write a critical essay on mass media or language, this book concentrates on the drama, prose and poetry options because these are the genres chosen most frequently.)

What the marker will be looking for

Your past paper books now contain marking schemes and so you can read for yourself the instructions that are given to markers. Markers are told to ensure that your essay is satisfactory in a number of main respects, known as the 'performance criteria' (or PCs). These criteria are the basis on which markers judge whether you have passed or failed.

- *PC 1: Understanding.* You must show secure understanding of key elements, central concerns and significant details of your texts, as appropriate to the task set in the question.

- *PC 2: Analysis.* In your essay you must explain accurately, and in detail, ways in which relevant aspects of structure/style/language contribute to the meaning/ effect/impact of your texts.

- *PC 3: Evaluation.* In your essay you must show clear engagement with the text or aspects of the text and state or imply an evaluation of its effectiveness, supported by detailed and relevant evidence from the text.

- *PC 4: Expression.* The structure of your essay and its style and language must communicate your meaning clearly and develop a line of thought that remains consistently relevant to the purpose. This includes the use of appropriate critical terminology. Your spelling, grammar and punctuation must be sufficiently accurate.

In order to pass, your essay must pass in *all* these performance criteria. The highest mark you can gain if any one of these criteria is not met is 11/25.

Part One

Preparing Your Texts

Choosing the Texts to Prepare

Getting Your Facts Right

Preparing the Evidence

The Mini Essay

Making Your Texts Manageable

Using Past Papers Wisely

Using Feedback Effectively

Choosing the Texts to Prepare

At school or college you will have studied literary texts within the main genres of drama, prose and poetry. This will give you sufficient choice for the Higher critical essay paper which requires you to write two essays, each from a different genre.

Depending on your course, you may have covered a wide variety of texts or just enough to enable you to write two essays from different sections. In most cases, however, you will have some choice as to the texts you eventually decide to concentrate on. At this stage, some candidates make a strategic error by narrowing their focus too much. They may give up on full-length texts and prepare poems or short stories only.

> I'm just doing one poem — but I'll learn it off by heart so I'll know it perfectly. Last year there was a question which would have suited it perfectly.

> I'm going to do a short story instead of my novel. I didn't really like the novel but the short story was very enjoyable.

> I'm not going to do **Macbeth** in the exam. There are so many quotations to learn and it's all a bit complicated.

> I'm doing the play but I'm only going to prepare a couple of scenes from it — there's usually a question on a scene.

Decisions like these can seriously jeopardise your chances of getting a good grade, or even of passing the exam.

What not to do

✘ **Don't** rely on a particular question from a past paper coming up again. It may not!

✘ **Don't** be overly influenced by whether you 'like' a text. It makes the task of preparation more enjoyable if you do, but the main requirement is that the text has the degree of complexity required to provide in-depth analysis, which will give proof of your ability.

✘ **Don't** just choose the easiest options. Short, simple texts will not always allow you to show your best work.

✘ **Don't** rule out a demanding text (such as a play by Shakespeare) just because you know it will require considerable commitment on your part to master it thoroughly. An examiner will always give you credit for making the effort.

✘ **Don't** skip parts of longer texts. Full-length texts such as novels and plays give you greater scope in choosing questions. However, while some questions may ask you to focus on a single scene or chapter, you will always have to show knowledge of the whole text.

✘ **Don't** expect a single short story or poem to be an 'all-purpose' text for its section. You may not get any question that is a suitable 'fit'. However well you know the texts, you will fail the essay if the text you choose is completely inappropriate for the question.

If you are undertaking Higher English with the aim of gaining a good grade, you should be able to cope with a reasonably wide range of reading. An acceptable bank of texts might be

- one play

- one full-length work of fiction or non-fiction or a book of short stories

- five poems (If two of the five poems were on the same theme and two were by the same poet, this would provide two units within this genre.)

In Part Two of this book you will be given advice on selecting questions. If you have not prepared a wide enough bank of texts, your ability to select will be seriously restricted and this will in turn restrict the chance you have to impress the examiners!

Getting Your Facts Right

Reading the texts

Markers are instructed to look for **'knowledge of the text'** when deciding whether to give a pass or fail mark. To be awarded a good grade, an essay must show **'thorough knowledge'**.

You must read all the texts that you plan to use for your critical essays. In the case of plays, poems and perhaps short stories, you may have the opportunity to hear these read aloud which is a great help towards understanding and learning. However, you should always try to make time to re-read your texts at home.

Showing your knowledge

'Showing' your knowledge does *not* mean retelling the plot of a text in your essay.

However, you must check that you can accurately recall

- the title (spelt correctly)
- the author's name (spelt correctly)
- names of characters and places (spelt correctly)
- the opening
- the ending.

Preparation Task 1

For each of the texts you are preparing for the examination, write down the answers to the five bullet points above.

You could use the photocopiable template on page 133 to record this information in a clear and easy-to-learn format.

Consolidating your knowledge

Having read your longer texts, you must then thoroughly familiarise yourself with the order in which events in the plot of a play or novel occur. It is not necessary to know the exact number of every scene or chapter, but it can be convenient to know one or two that are important to the text. For example, the scene in which Romeo kills Tybalt in *Romeo and Juliet* is Act 3 Scene 1.

In the case of poems and short stories, you must develop a clear awareness of the **structure** of ideas or events.

Preparation Task 2

Compile a scene-by-scene or chapter-by-chapter summary of each of your longer texts. The briefer your summaries are, the better. If possible, try to present the plan of the whole text on a single page.

You could also compile similar plans to show the structure of short stories or poems.

Example: This is a summary of Act 1 of *Macbeth*.

If you were to summarise all the acts in *Macbeth* equally briefly, you would have an at-a-glance synopsis of the whole play on a single page:

Act 1	Scene 1	the witches in the storm
	Scene 2	the report of the battle
	Scene 3	the witches' promises to Macbeth
	Scene 4	Malcolm made Prince of Cumberland
	Scene 5	Lady Macbeth reads Macbeth's letter
	Scene 6	Duncan arrives at Macbeth's castle
	Scene 7	Macbeth is persuaded to murder Duncan

As an aid to memory, it can be helpful to colour, highlight or illustrate these single-page plans. As you do so, you will gradually assimilate the information they contain.

The 'central concerns'

The knowledge mentioned above must be committed accurately to memory. However, it is just the foundation. It is crucial that you also show *understanding* of the 'central concerns', which are the *ideas* contained in the text.

Central concerns of a text might include the following:

- Themes, such as love; revenge; mortality; ambition; the appreciation of beauty; good and evil.

- Social issues, such as social class; family life; corruption in society.

- Characters and their personalities: how they interact and influence one another; what motivates characters or causes them to change and develop.

Your 'line of thought'

When you come to write your essay, you will not be expected to cover every aspect of the text. Because you have just 45 minutes in which to write the essay, it will be essential to select only what is relevant to the question you have chosen. The question will set out a particular task. You must then try to carry out the task, keeping to a particular 'line of thought' and not diverging from it.

This is known as the **'argument'** or 'topic' of your essay. Each of the questions will direct you to adopt a particular 'line of thought'. (Advice on how to do this is given in Part Two of this book.)

In order to be able to carry out such a task effectively, you must not only know your texts thoroughly and understand the ideas they contain but also be able to provide **evidence** for what you say.

The assessment criteria, which can be found on the critical essay paper, spell out clearly the requirement for **'detailed and relevant evidence'** to support any statements you make concerning the ideas and style of the text and the evaluation you make of it.

Preparing the Evidence

The strategies suggested in Preparation Tasks 1 and 2 will help you to build up an accurate knowledge of the texts you are preparing for the critical essay paper. You will also have discussed and thought about the ideas contained in the texts that will form the foundations of the lines of thought you will present in your essays.

You must now consider *how* you will provide the 'detailed and relevant' evidence that the assessment criteria demand. Some of your evidence will take the form of arguments and explanations, and you may also simply refer to parts of the text. For example, you might comment that Shakespeare's *Macbeth* begins with a storm, and this disturbance in the weather symbolises a disturbance in the human world.

However, it will also be essential to use **quotations**. Direct quotation is absolutely vital in the discussion of poetry, the genre in which language is most sensitive, but it is also important in the accurate and effective analysis of drama and prose.

> 'I think there is no sense in forming an opinion when there is no evidence to form it on. If you build a person without any bones in him he may look fair enough to the eye, but he cannot stand up; and I consider that evidence is the bones of an opinion.'
>
> *(Mark Twain, 1835–1910)*

Selecting quotations

The more quotations you can commit to memory, the more lines of argument you will be able to support successfully. Remember that these quotations will be used as *evidence* to back up what you say when you **analyse** your texts. A quotation should not be used merely to show that you have learned it. You should therefore select quotations that will help you to illustrate a particular aspect of the text.

For example, this could be one of the central concerns mentioned earlier, which include themes, social issues or characters. Alternatively, it could be a literary device such as setting, symbolism or imagery. Quotation is essential if you wish to demonstrate precisely the author's use of language, for example in word choice, sentence structure or any figure of speech involving sound, such as alliteration.

Tip!

Although many people refer to quotations using the abbreviation 'quotes', you should not do this in your essay. Correctly used, the word 'quote' is a verb. Introduce your quotation with a comment, *not* with:

'Here is a quote…'

✗

Preparation Task 3

Compile a bank of quotations from each of your chosen texts.

A good way to set out a bank of quotations is to divide your page into two. You can then write comments in the box opposite. The comments will refer to whatever aspect of the text you feel the words illustrate. An example from Shakespeare's *Macbeth* is shown below.

Quotation	Comment
Macbeth Act 1 Scene 2 'What bloody man is that?' (line 1)	*The phrase 'bloody man', which refers to the wounded captain, begins a theme. The imagery of blood will permeate the play and the most 'bloody man' will be Macbeth himself.*
'His brandish'd steel…smoked with bloody execution' (lines 17–18)	*'Smoked' refers to the way the warm blood of his slaughtered enemies steams on Macbeth's sword blade. This, together with the word 'bloody', conveys horrible brutality, and contrasts with the more heroic, romantic image of the character in 'brandish'd steel'.*

If you do this task on a computer you can expand or add to your comments at later revision sessions.

It is sensible to provide line or page references, as in the example above, so that you can check back to the context of the quotations at any time.

Two points to remember:

- Ideally, quotations should be no longer than *two lines* of verse or around *twelve words* of prose. Short *phrases* or even *single words* can also provide effective evidence.

- Choose quotations that make complete sense.

For example, in Act 1 Scene 7 of Macbeth, it would not make sense to quote line 32 by itself:

> He hath honoured me of late, and I have bought

This is an example of enjambment, where the sense of the line runs on to the next, with the following line necessary to complete the sense:

> He hath honoured me of late, and I have bought
> Golden opinions from all sorts of people.

However, this quotation includes two clauses, and you could use either clause on its own:

> He hath honoured me of late.

or

> ...I have bought
> Golden opinions from all sorts of people.

Macbeth and Lady Macbeth

Each of these makes sense by itself and could be used to illustrate a point of analysis.

You should always try to quote from drama and poetry in the original lines, using the correct line breaks as shown above. An alternative way to show the line break is to use the slash symbol:

> I have bought/Golden opinions from all sorts of people.

In addition, you may use ellipsis (...) to edit quotations so that they will make sense without being too long. For example:

> Come, you spirits...unsex me here.

Here, lines 42–43 from *Macbeth* Act 1 Scene 5 are amalgamated to give the gist of Lady Macbeth's words.

It is also acceptable to exchange certain words such as pronouns to fit the quotations into your essay. It is usual to put such changes in brackets, set out as in the following example:

Lady Macbeth calls on the 'spirits that tend on mortal thoughts' to 'unsex [her]'.

The word 'her' replaces the word 'me' in the text because the character is referred to in the third person, whereas in the original the character speaks in the first person.

Because of techniques such as rhythm and rhyme, it is easier to learn quotations from poetry and drama than extracts from prose. It is therefore advisable to select phrases rather than complete sentences from prose unless you have a particularly good memory. In addition, if you quote at great length you will reduce the amount of time you have to write your analysis.

Your teacher may provide a list of quotations for you. However, it will be to your advantage to add to it or to make your own personal collection. Choosing your own will make your essay original. Moreover, the process of selecting quotations and writing them down will help you to remember them.

Organising your banks of quotations

You will find it very helpful to group your banks of quotations into topics. The purpose behind this is to enable you to see how flexibly your knowledge can be applied. It will be very important when writing your critical essay to select *only what is relevant to the questions*.

Tip!

Try to select quotations that are interesting in both **ideas** and **expression**.

Such topics might include

- the development of one character
- the relationship between two characters
- themes
- setting(s)
- imagery (different themes could be grouped separately)
- symbols
- narrative methods.

The more topics and subtopics you can think of, the better.

Remember that many quotations may be 'multi-purpose' – they can be used to illustrate several different aspects of the text.

If you have compiled a scene-by-scene or chapter-by-chapter bank of quotations, you can use various methods to group them. You could have a colour coding system using highlighters.

If you have your bank of quotations saved on your computer, you could use cut-and-paste to select those quotations that illustrate the various topics and create a separate file for each. Remember to give each file a clear heading to remind you what the theme is for that particular group of quotations.

Preparation Task 4

Organise your banks of quotations thematically, as suggested above.

Learning the quotations

You are unlikely to learn your quotations just by reading them.

Preparation Task 5

Try the 'look and copy' strategy until you are word perfect. Look at the words for around 10 or 15 seconds, cover them up and write them down on paper. Repeat this until you can write them perfectly. Try again a few days later. Each time you will be able to learn the quotation more quickly. An alternative technique that some people find helpful is to make an audio recording of your own voice and play it back to yourself. Keep repeating the quotations until you get them right.

Summing up: some do's and don'ts of providing evidence:

Do... ✔	Don't... ✗
Quote as briefly as possible in order to make your point.	Quote whole verses of poetry or many lines of plays and prose.
Quote in grammatically complete units that make sense. (This is explained on page 9.)	Quote fragments of sentences that don't make sense.
Quote only to support a point of analysis. There is no point in using a quotation to provide a summary of your text.	Give the evidence before you make the comment.
	Use the same quotation more than once in an essay. This suggests that your knowledge is rather thin.
If possible, back up your point with a second piece of evidence.	Say 'Here is a quotation…' or (even worse!) 'Here is a quote…'
Make sure your quotations are actually illustrating what you have said.	Quote words that only vaguely relate to your comment.

The Mini Essay

Another useful revision strategy is the so-called 'mini' essay.

A mini essay is an essay of 200–300 words (two or three paragraphs) that targets a particular aspect of the text. For example, a mini essay could analyse what makes the opening scene of a play gripping, or what captures the reader's interest in the first paragraph of a novel or short story.

You could consider some of the following topics, or your teacher may suggest topics that refer directly to the texts you are studying.

Mini-essay topics

- The way a character is introduced in a play, novel or short story.

- How setting relates to the theme.

- How symbolism of colour or the weather is used.

- The significance of a particular episode or scene.

- The author's use of contrast.

- The use of dialect or direct speech.

- The role of the narrator in a prose text.

- A poet's use of techniques of sound.

It is advisable to do more shorter mini essays than fewer longer ones for two reasons:

✔ You will only need to allocate around 20 minutes of your time to produce each short piece.

✔ Many short pieces will give you the flexibility you need to be able to focus clearly on the exam questions. You will have detailed knowledge of many different aspects of your text.

Sample mini essay

Text: *Macbeth* by William Shakespeare

Aspect: The impact of the opening scene of the play

— —

The play opens with thunder and lightning. These striking stage effects shock the audience and prepare them for a disturbing drama to follow. The tension is raised further by the appearance of three witches who, according to the text, should be grotesquely ugly in appearance, old women with beards, who are 'withered and wild in their attire'. They are clearly creatures of another world, indicating that the supernatural will be an element of the play. The heath on which they appear is traditionally a wilderness cut off from the civilised world, where evil may flourish unchecked. Atmosphere is built up by the witches' references to their familiars, 'Graymalkin' (the cat) and 'Paddock' (the toad). In Elizabethan folklore such animals were thought to embody evil spirits who would do the bidding of witches.

A storm is often symbolic of disorder in the human world, and this application is confirmed by the mention of a battle. The theme of winning and losing is introduced in the words, 'when the battle's lost and won'. The unearthly power of the witches is shown by their knowledge of the future – they know the battle will be over by 'set of sun'. The witches state that they intend to 'meet with Macbeth'. The audience is intrigued to know what connection Macbeth can have with them and why they wish to meet him. The fact that his name is on the tongues of the evil witches links him with evil. The final chant of the witches, 'Fair is foul and foul is fair', begins another theme that will be important to the drama: false appearance. The alliteration of the soft, sinister 'f' sounds has a chilling effect that fills the audience with foreboding. (286 words)

Preparation Task 6

Compile a bank of mini essays on each of your texts. (Each piece should take no more than 20 minutes.)

Making Your Texts Manageable

Preparing one or more full-length texts to exam standard can seem like a very daunting task. However, there are ways to approach your revision that can help you master them.

Drama

It goes without saying that if you're studying a play for your English exam you will have to read it from start to finish and thoroughly familiarise yourself with all aspects of it.

However, when you write a critical essay on a play, it is not possible to discuss every scene or speech in detail. Some candidates attempt to do this and they are almost always unsuccessful. They will either cover the whole text too thinly, or else they will not get much beyond the first act.

You should therefore focus your revision on what are known as **'key scenes'**. Key scenes are those that are important to the drama as a whole and that clearly illustrate the central concerns outlined on page 6. The first and last scenes are very likely to fall into this category, as are any scenes where the plot develops significantly or where the characters do or say something that is very important to your understanding of the issues of the play.

The bulk of your essay will present evidence from these scenes, although you must also show knowledge of the whole play.

Preparation Task 7

Prepare a commentary on each key scene of your text based on the following model from *Romeo and Juliet*, Act 3 Scene 1. In the first column, list each main event in the scene. In the second column, make notes relating the event to a theme or any other central concern. In the third column, comment on what the event reveals about the characters. A photocopiable template is on page 134.

Title ___Romeo and Juliet___   Author ___William Shakespeare___

Drama scene commentary   Act ___3___   Scene ___1___

Event	Themes/ideas	Characterisation
Benvolio tries to persuade Mercutio to go home in case they meet the Capulets, whom he knows are roaming around. He knows that the heat will intensify their emotions. Mercutio carelessly dismisses his fears with jokes.	Conflict: the feud casts its shadow over the love story throughout. The hot weather symbolises the hot tempers, which will flare up with fatal consequences.	Benvolio personifies goodwill. However, his 'good will' will be eclipsed by the forces of ill will. Mercutio acts as a catalyst: his humour will provoke Tybalt.
Tybalt arrives. He speaks politely, calling the Montagues 'gentlemen' and asks to talk to them. However, Mercutio replies aggressively.	Tybalt is the force for violence and disorder in the play. The audience is aware that he swore to change the atmosphere from 'seeming sweet' to 'bitterest gall'.	Tybalt's politeness seems unconvincing. The audience know that Mercutio's taunting will enrage him even more.
Romeo arrives and ignores Tybalt's challenge. He is newly married and in high spirits. He is no longer interested in pursuing the feud.	Love is opposed to violence. Romeo tries to deflect Tybalt's aggression with talk of love. However, the audience is aware of how strong Tybalt's grudge against Romeo is.	The audience knows that Tybalt will react angrily. As in the balcony scene, Romeo uses rather poetic, playful language; this will backfire because Tybalt does not understand the context.

Plays in performance

If possible, you should take the opportunity to see a live performance of your drama text. In addition to aiding your understanding, this will provide an overview of the complete text. Live performances are striking because of their use of costumes, music and stage sets, all of which help to impress the text on your memory and sharpen your appreciation of the central concerns. However, you should not attempt to make a particular performance the focus of an entire essay unless your teacher has prepared you especially for this.

What about watching the films?

Films can bring a text to life in an enjoyable and instructive way. However, you should not focus an essay directly on a film unless you have been specifically trained for a film question, which will require you to demonstrate technical knowledge of things like camera angles and editing procedures. Also, remember that films often alter and cut the texts. Polanski's *Macbeth*, for example, has Banquo's ghost entering only once, and cuts completely the section of Act 4 Scene 3 where Malcolm tests Macduff. This sequence contains significant ideas on one of the main themes of the play: the topic of what makes an ideal king.

Preparation Task 8

Watch a film of your text, either alone or with others. Make notes on the changes the director has made to the original text. Discuss how these changes affect your understanding of the play. You could discuss with your group how far you feel such changes or cuts affect your appreciation.

Prose

In the case of full-length works of fiction or non-fiction, it will not be possible to provide blanket coverage of the whole book in a critical essay written in under an hour. You will have to select key episodes or chapters that you can use to illustrate your arguments.

Try to identify incidents that are particularly significant. The opening and the ending are likely to fall into this category, as are any episodes in which significant plot developments occur.

Preparation Task 9

Prepare revision sheets on key episodes in your novel. In the same way, you can prepare sheets on complete short stories you have studied. In the first column, list each main event in the episode. In the second column, make notes relating the event to a theme or any other central concern. In the third column, make notes on what the event reveals about the characters. A photocopiable template is on page 135.

The following model is from the opening of Chapter 1 of *The Changeling* by Robin Jenkins. The plot of the novel involves a teacher offering a holiday to a pupil from a poor home, but by doing so he hopes to gain promotion.

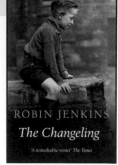

Title ___The Changeling___ Author ___Robin Jenkins___

Prose commentary Chapter/episode ___1___

Event	Themes/ideas	Characterisation
The 'Good Samaritan' is mentioned, but with the ironic comment that he did not have anyone to warn him of the 'folly of interference'.	Altruism: the difficulty of doing good in isolation without affecting people in unexpected, negative ways.	Charlie Forbes is identified with an archetypal example of the good Christian, which makes a favourable initial impression on the reader.
Charlie Forbes praises Tom Curdie's essay on 'The Sea'. He notes the great intelligence of Tom, although Tom is dressed like 'a little scarecrow' and comes from a notorious slum. Tom meekly accepts the patronising comments and endures the sneers of his better-off classmates.	Social inequality and injustice. Tom is isolated among his classmates. The contrast of his dirty rags with their 'crested blazers' is visual evidence of this.	Tom has a high intellect, and is brave and stoical in the face of his classmates' snobbish treatment of him. Although Charlie means well, he seems rather conceited in comparing what he sees as his own tolerant attitude with the other teachers' disapproval of Tom.

Poetry

If you are writing a critical essay on a poem, you will be expected to show thorough knowledge of the whole text. Unless the poem is an exceptionally long, narrative text, your analysis will cover all parts of the poem.

A useful revision technique is to make several copies of the text. You can then annotate these in different ways, using one for ideas, one for imagery, one for other poetic techniques and so on.

Here is an example of this, using the first verse only of the poem 'Hands' by Ted Hughes.

Ideas

Hands seem to represent man himself: tough, efficient and competent

Emphasis on large size – connotations of strength

Hands taken for granted – suggests modesty and stoical nature of man

Seem to show no pain, as if they are made of something other than flesh and blood

---

Hands

Your hands were strange – huge.

A farmer's joke: 'still got your bloody great hands!'

You used them with as little regard

As old iron tools – as if their creased, glossed, crocodile leather

Were nerveless, like an African's footsoles.

Imagery

Simile 'as old iron tools' suggests hands are tough and indestructible, lacking any feeling – plain and ordinary

'Crocodile leather' metaphor suggests appearance of hands – very brown, creased and thick-skinned

'Like an African's footsoles': slightly comic simile but emphasises hardness from going barefoot, suggests palms of hands toughened by constant use

---

Techniques

Poem is written in the second person, as if addressing the farmer ('your...'), although he is dead

Poem is like a tribute to him as this sets up a respectful tone

Placing 'huge' in stress position at end of line and sentence gives impact; suggests sense of awe, perhaps as it from the point of view of a child

Direct speech in line 2 gives the poem a colloquial style, as if the poet is thinking aloud

Unrhymed, free verse also gives impression of spontaneous thought

> ### Preparation Task 10
>
> Annotate copies of your chosen poems based on the model of Ted Hughes'
> 'Hands' on page 19. It is advisable to separate your comments into literary topics
> in this way rather than try to write everything on one copy of the poem, which
> will soon become overcrowded with writing and illegible.

A poetry 'bank'

If you intend to write on poetry, it will be important to prepare a range of texts from a variety of periods and styles. This will avoid the common situation of a candidate twisting and distorting a text when trying to answer a question for which the poem is not appropriate. Preparing a poetry 'bank' will ensure that you can choose a question that will enable you to demonstrate your critical skills to their full potential.

A suitable bank of poems might begin with some thematically linked poems by contemporary writers. For example, Carol Ann Duffy's poems 'In Mrs Tilscher's Class' and 'Originally' could be studied alongside Liz Lochhead's 'Revelation' or Kate Clanchy's 'Timetable'. In Duffy's poems, she deals with the balance of pain and excitement in growing up. Themes of change, personal identity and education are also explored, all of which are relevant to teenagers. The poems are unrhymed and use deceptively simple, colloquial language, but include vivid imagery and striking use of sound. 'Revelation' and 'Timetable' explore similar themes and would offer various significant points of comparison in style. Such a group of poems would enable you to answer a question about the comparison of works either by the same writer or by different writers.

Because these poems are all by contemporary writers, you should add one or two pre-twentieth century poems to your bank. Robert Browning's dramatic monologues offer a fascinating insight into evil and warped minds, while often including an element of black comedy or the macabre that is entertaining to the reader. Titles include 'My Last Duchess', 'Porphyria's Lover' and 'Soliloquy of the Spanish Cloister'. Although they were written more than a hundred years ago, their themes of love, pride and jealousy remain relevant for all time.

While Browning's monologues would fulfil the categories of specific genres and also poems depicting people, it would be useful to include at least one descriptive poem in your bank. A suitable example might be George Mackay Brown's 'Hamnavoe', a delightful evocation of life in the town of Stromness in Orkney around a century ago; it is also a tribute to the poet's father. A poem with a focus on nature would also be a good choice. The ode 'To Autumn', by the Romantic poet John Keats, also deals with interesting themes of change and mortality, and the richness of its language repays close study. You could compare it to some of the nature poems of the American writer Robert Frost, which also show the cycle of nature in relation to human life.

It would also be advisable to include one of the longer, narrative poems in your bank. Examples of entertaining storytelling in verse include Robert Burns' *Tam o' Shanter* and Keats' *The Eve of St Agnes*. Both poems are vividly atmospheric, with Burns providing a comic tale of a drunken Scotsman's encounter with witches and Keats a Romantic, medieval love story.

Tam o'Shanter

Using Past Papers Wisely

Once you have prepared notes on all your texts you can then look at the questions that have been asked in past papers and practise writing essays that answer them.

There are two main ways in which to do this.

You can write a practice essay as homework, taking as much time as you need. You will be able to refer to your text and notes as you prepare a response to the question you have chosen. Such a task will enable you to think more deeply about your text and help imprint it on your memory. It will also give you practice in planning your answer because you can spend time doing this properly.

Alternatively, you may be given the opportunity to write an essay under timed, exam conditions without text or notes. This is also a useful form of preparation. A timed exercise will enable you to discover your own capabilities in terms of what you can write in the time allowed, and how well you know your text. Such practice will train you to plan quickly and to write without making too many changes.

What not to do

Read the story of Lucy, who was hoping to do well in her English exam:

Does this seem like a story with a happy ending?

Lucy feels optimistic that she is going to do well.

However, this story is likely to have a sting in the tail:

Sadly, it is likely that when the results come out, Lucy will not have gained a very good grade even though she worked so hard. She may have had to tackle a question for which she was not well prepared, or she may have gone ahead and written 'her' essay as the answer to another question. In the latter case, she will have been marked down for irrelevance.

Aiming to perfect one essay topic in the hope it will appear in the exam that you will be sitting is *not* a good idea, and will lead to frustration in the long run. However, you can gain a great deal from looking at the questions that have been asked in previous years. This will give you an idea of the range of the questions.

Tip!

Never put yourself in a position to say, 'My question did not come up'.

Using Feedback Effectively

The story of Lucy was an illustration of how *not* to use feedback from your teacher. However, it is equally unwise to ignore your teacher's comments and just look at your mark. Many pupils are interested only in their mark and how it compares with the marks of others in the class. Your mark is not unimportant, because it gives an indication of how far you are satisfying the performance criteria, but at this stage it is less important than thinking over the comments.

In the scenario in the cartoon strip, Lucy went wrong at frame 3. After receiving her essay back, what she should have done was to translate Mr Stuart's comments into *general* advice.

For example, if her teacher had written, 'There was no need to give a full account of all of the witches' prophecies at the start', instead of rewriting her entire essay, excluding the account of the witches' prophecies, she could have simply made a note of a general criticism:

> ## Tip!
> Repeatedly redrafting one essay is rarely the best use of your revision time.

✗ There was too much retelling of the plot.

Focus on the comments, not the mark

It is good practice to have a sheet on which you record both marks and teachers' comments, add your own comment (in which you generalise on the teacher's point) and set targets for future writing. It could look something like this:

Date	Assignment
3 Jan	*Practice critical essay on 'Macbeth' past paper 2005 (question 4)*

Mark	Teacher's comment
14/25	Although you showed good knowledge, you tended to wander off the topic when you discussed Lady Macbeth's soliloquy on Macbeth's character and ambition. You had plenty of good ideas on the issue of 'dark or pessimistic' elements of the play and it was good that you used these words frequently. However, you wasted time by giving too many details of what Macbeth did – brief summaries would have been enough to show why the mood was 'appropriate'.
	My comment
	Focus on the words of the question. Avoid retelling the plot so much.

A photocopiable template for your own use is on page 136.

Preparation Task 11

Read the teacher's comments on the opening few paragraphs of Lucy's essay, below. Then make a list of the *general* advice she could have derived from them. The comments are numbered, and you should be able to make one general piece of advice from each numbered comment. The first one is given to start you off.

Question:

Choose a play in which the mood is mainly dark or pessimistic.

Show how the dramatist creates this mood and discuss how appropriate it is to the main idea(s) of the play.

Lucy's essay

1. I like the way you repeat the words of the question in your opening sentence.

3. No need to give a blow-by-blow account of everything Macbeth does. A brief explanation that he murders the king would be enough at this stage.

A play in which the mood is mainly dark or pessimistic is *Macbeth* by William Shakespeare. The play is about a Scottish nobleman, Macbeth, who meets three witches who promise he will become the Thane of Cawdor and then king: 'king hereafter'. Macbeth writes and tells his ambitious wife, Lady Macbeth, about the promises. She is full of excited anticipation, but she thinks Macbeth is too kind to murder the present king, Duncan:

> 'Yet do I fear thy nature
> It is too full of the milk of human kindness
> To catch the nearest way. Thou wouldst be great,
> Art not without ambition, but without
> The illness should attend it.'

2. What is the point of this quotation about being king? No need to quote in a summary.

4. This quotation is far too long. In any case, you have not related it to the topic of the 'dark and pessimistic mood'.

→

It seems she is right when Macbeth in a soliloquy decides it would be quite wrong to carry out the murder. 'He's here in double trust.' However, she persuades him to go ahead and he does so. After murdering Duncan, Macbeth is full of guilt but he goes on to murder his friend, Banquo, then the wife and children of Macduff and many of his other enemies too. Finally, at the end of the play, Macduff and Duncan's son Malcolm defeat Macbeth in battle.

5. You are digressing here, and also retelling too much of the plot. Some explanation of the context is needed, but you are giving far too much detail. The quotation from the soliloquy is not needed and is just holding you up from getting to grips with the main topic of the question.

6. At last you have got on to the topic! A good, relevant paragraph. I like the way you show awareness of the drama genre by mentioning the 'audience'.

The mood of darkness is set up in the opening scene with the witches on the heath. The storm suggests it is literally dark, and this hints at evil and disorder, which is appropriate in a play about treachery and murder. Witches are universally recognised as evil creatures and the audience will at once sense the mood of a play that they introduce will be dark.

Points of general advice

1   Always repeat the key words of the question in the opening sentence of your essay.

2   ....

3   ....

4   ....

5   ....

6   ....

Compare your suggestions to those given on page 28.

The texts and beyond

In order to understand the central concerns of the texts, it is helpful to read more widely. Read and annotate the introductions to your texts, which will often give you useful information. It can also be helpful to read other works by the same author so that you gain a clear impression of the author's style and ideas.

There are many editions of student notes covering the texts you are likely to be studying. You may find these helpful as an additional aid to understanding aspects of your texts. However, you must use them with caution. Do not be tempted simply to learn sample essays or extracts from the notes and pass them off as your own work. This is called *plagiarism*, and is dishonest. If a marker recognises that you have done this it could lead to your certificate being withheld.

And finally…re-read your texts!

Most people preparing for exams will pore over their notes for hours, but it is surprising how few people think of sitting down and just reading over their texts one more time. In the case of a poem, this will take a few minutes; a play will take an hour or two. A full-length book will take longer, but it is very worthwhile: you will gain a valuable overview after studying incidents in a more fragmentary way.

Suggested answers to exercise on Lucy's essay (pages 26–27)

1   Always repeat the key words of the question in the opening sentence of your essay.

2   Do not use quotations in your introduction. Do not use any quotation merely to summarise. Only include a quotation to illustrate a point of analysis.

3   A short summary of the text is all that is required in your introduction. If possible, limit it to a single sentence.

4   Do not quote long sections of text. Quote only the minimum amount that will make sense while still making your point. Again, only use quotations that illustrate some point in the main argument. The whole of this quotation is unnecessary, because it is unrelated to the topic of 'dark and pessimistic mood'.

5   Do not digress onto different topics, however well you know them. Do not slip into retelling the whole plot. Only give enough to provide a context for your discussion.

6   Include the key words of the topic as often as possible.

Part Two
Writing the Essay

The Formula

Alice was preparing for her Highers, and writing a practice critical essay:

> Alice was writing an essay on Robert Browning. Pinned up in front of her was a calendar with black lines through the days of the year that had already elapsed. Boxed in red was the week of her Higher exams. The narrowing down of the clean white days between the red days and the encroaching black-lined ones made a crawling fear quicken in her stomach. This morning, when she was walking up to school, she'd felt the prickling smart in her throat and nose that meant hayfever, and hayfever meant summer and summer meant exams.
>
> Alice bent her head over her work again. 'Compare and contrast,' the question read, 'the motivation of the Duke in "My Last Duchess" and those of the monk in "Fra Lippo Lippi".' Alice had four pages of notes and an essay plan. There was, she knew, a formula to these things: an introductory paragraph in which you should answer the question in shortened form and explain your argument, an expansion on your argument – using at all times as many quotes as you could, as well as, where possible, the words of the question – a final paragraph where you could try and crowbar in as many other insights as you had about this text, if you had any, and then a summing-up, referring back to your introduction. It should be easy, it should be easy. But she couldn't quell these nerves. At night, she lay awake thinking over revision plans, subjects, notes, diagrams, links, multiple-choice answers.
>
> From *After You'd Gone* by Maggie O'Farrell

Alice's 'formula' is on the right lines, even if she does call her quotations 'quotes'!

You can help quell those nerves by learning the correct strategies for critical essay writing.

Reading the Question

Having completed your preparation you should now, like Alice, be ready to write the essay.

The first step to a good mark is to read the questions carefully!

Each question will ask you to do two things:

- Choose a suitable text for the question.
- Carry out the task the question asks you to do.

Under the stress of exam conditions, the biggest temptation is to choose the first possible question and then to write down everything you know about the text you have prepared. Try to resist this! If you can force yourself to take your time and then make a reasoned choice, it is likely that you will achieve a better result.

Choosing the right text

At the very beginning of the critical essay paper you are told how your essay will be assessed. The first of these criteria is '*the relevance of your essays to the questions you have chosen*'. This shows that choosing the right question is of the utmost importance.

Tip!

Do not restrict your choice of questions by preparing too few texts.

Each question in the critical essay paper will begin by asking you to 'choose' a text of some kind.

Drama

Drama questions will all begin with the requirement to:

> Choose a play…

It is likely that you will have prepared only one play, and so you will not, in fact, have a choice of texts. But, while the same play will probably be an appropriate text for several questions, it will be important for you to choose the question in which you can gain the best mark. This is discussed on pages 34–35.

Prose

In the case of *prose*, you must have a clear knowledge of whether your text is *fiction* or *non-fiction*. If you choose a non-fiction question for a text that is actually fiction, or vice versa, your essay will be severely penalised, no matter how good your analysis is.

In the case of prose fiction, you will be directed to

> Choose a novel or short story…

As with drama, it is likely that you will have only one full-length prose work to choose from. You must look carefully at the description of the novel you are asked to choose and think about whether your novel will fit. For example, one of the 2007 questions asked for 'a novel with an ending that you found unexpected'. This is more suited to some texts than others, so it would not necessarily be a good choice. Questions on short stories are likely to be more limiting than those on novels.

The *non-fiction* questions will ask you to 'choose a non-fiction text' or they will specify a subgenre of non-fiction, such as biography. In the 2007 paper, one non-fiction question included what is called a 'closed list' of subjects, which does not allow other possibilities to be used. The topics specified were 'travel or exploration or discovery'. This restricted choice might rule out your text.

Poetry

In the poetry section of the 2005 paper, one question began like this:

> Choose a poem that you feel is particularly relevant to a teenage audience.

What sort of poem might this be? A poem about childhood or adolescence, perhaps, or about relationships? 'Tich Miller' by Wendy Cope, with themes of disability and bullying, or Simon Armitage's 'I Am Very Bothered', on teenage love, are particularly relevant to teenagers, as is Liz Lochhead's 'Revelation', about loss of childhood innocence. You might also make a case for a poem on war, because young servicemen and victims of war are often people with whom teenagers can identify.

However, many poems that are frequently studied in school would not be suitable. If you were to answer this question on John Keats' 'To Autumn', a poem that looks at time and mortality through the changing seasons, you would be unlikely to gain a top mark, however perceptive and accurate your analysis, because it would be difficult to make a case for its having a *particular* relevance to teenagers.

While you must be ready to expect some questions that offer a limited choice of texts in this way, the poetry section usually contains at least one question that offers a wider choice. An example from 2007 asked you to:

> Choose a poem in which there is effective use of one or more of the following: verse form, rhythm, rhyme, repetition, sound.

Because these technical features are common to all poetry, *any* poem could have been chosen.

Tip!

Do not choose a poetry question unless you can write on a poem that is *completely* appropriate.

For Practice 1

1 Look at the Poetry section of the critical essay paper for any one year in your past papers booklet. Consider how suitable the texts you have prepared would be using the following scale. You can do this exercise individually, but it is even more useful to do it in a pair or group.

1	My text is totally unsuitable. I could not do this question.
2	My text is not really suitable. I would do this question only if all the others were impossible.
3	My text would do, but it is not the most obvious or natural choice.
4	My text fits this question fairly well.
5	My text is a perfect match.

2 Write a sentence about each question, justifying where you placed it on the scale.

If you have been doing this as a group exercise, you can now compare your answers to both tasks with other groups.

Warning!

It is worth repeating here that a *full-length* literary work such as a play or a novel should offer you enough flexibility to have a choice of questions in the section, provided you have prepared the text thoroughly. However, there is no such thing as an 'all-purpose' poem or short story. Many candidates choose such a text because in the short term it seems an easier option: they feel more confident of remembering it under exam conditions. However, if you prepare one such text only, you may find that there is *no* question for which it is an appropriate choice.

Choosing the right question

Questions vary in difficulty, and while you will get credit for making a good attempt at a demanding question, it makes sense to choose questions that will give you the best chance of impressing the examiner.

In the case of poetry, your choice is likely to be dictated by the need to find a question that fits your text. In the case of drama and prose, there may be more than one question that you can choose. Always read *all* the questions – do not rush to make a start on the first question that seems possible. Then take a few minutes to think about how you might answer each of the questions for which your text is a good 'fit'.

As an example, look at the four questions in the 2007 drama section:

> 1. Choose a play which has a theme of revenge or betrayal or sacrifice. Show how the dramatist explores your chosen theme and discuss how this treatment enhances your appreciation of the play as a whole.
>
> 2. Choose from a play an important scene that you found entertaining or particularly shocking. Explain briefly why the scene is important to the play as a whole and discuss in detail how the dramatist makes the scene so entertaining or shocking.
>
> 3. Choose a play in which a character makes a crucial error. Explain what the error is and discuss to what extent it is important to your understanding of the character's situation in the play as whole.
>
> 4. Choose a play in which the relationship between a male and a female character changes significantly. Show how the relationship between the two characters changes and discuss to what extent this illuminates a central idea of the play.

Suppose you had prepared Shakespeare's *Romeo and Juliet* as your text.

✗ The first question might seem a possible choice, but it would not be a particularly easy task to discuss any of these themes in relation to *Romeo and Juliet* although the play contains elements of all three.

✔ The second question would be straightforward. As a tragedy, the play offers several 'shocking' scenes. Act 3 Scene 1 (the fight scene) or Act 3 Scene 5 (where Juliet's father threatens to disown her) would make suitable choices. Alternatively, you could make a good case for the balcony scene (Act 2 Scene 2) being 'entertaining'. However, you would have to remember to explain why the scene was important to the play as a whole, in addition to your analysis of what made the scene 'shocking' or 'entertaining'.

✔ The third question would have been another very suitable choice. Your 'crucial error' could be Romeo's decision to intervene in the fight between Mercutio and Tybalt which leads to Tybalt's death. This would lead logically to further discussion of Romeo's impulsive character and the fateful consequences of the feud between the Montagues and Capulets.

✔ The last question would also be a good choice for *Romeo and Juliet*. However, you would then have to think carefully about which two characters to choose. Some candidates might go for the obvious choice of the lovers. A better choice might be the relationship between Juliet and her father. Choosing the lovers would be likely to result in a narrative of meeting – falling in love – being separated by Romeo's banishment. An essay on Juliet and Lord Capulet could analyse the reasons for their relationship changing from affection to extreme conflict.

For Practice 2

Assess the suitability of the drama questions listed on page 34 in relation to your own drama text. Rank them in order, and consider what scenes or characters you would choose. You could discuss this with a partner or group.

Focusing on the task

The second part of the question will set your task. Some candidates make the error of looking carefully at the first part of the question only. They choose a text that fits the question, but then virtually ignore the actual task and proceed to write a general

> **Tip!**
>
> The single most common fault in the critical essay is failure to focus on the question asked.

commentary based on notes or even a pre-prepared essay they have practised writing. (Look back at the cartoon strip on pages 23–24, which warned you against doing this!)

In the 2005 question which asked you to choose 'a poem of particular relevance to a teenage audience', the task required you to focus on the teenage appeal of the text:

> Make clear why you think the poem is so relevant to this age group and show how the poetic techniques used in the poem help to achieve this.

Even if you had chosen a suitable text such as those suggested on page 32, unless your essay concentrated on *why the poem appealed especially to teenagers* and *how the poetic techniques contributed to this*, your analysis would not be judged to be 'appropriate to the task' by the examiner. Unless you focus precisely on the task, you will not get a top mark.

Be wary also of questions that offer a wide choice of texts. This may suggest to you that the task will be easy. In the 2007 poetry question, which asked you to choose a poem that used one or more of 'verse form, rhythm, rhyme, repetition and sound' effectively, the task was to:

> Show how the poet effectively uses the feature(s) to enhance your appreciation of the poem as a whole.

Although this question gave the candidate a wide choice of texts, the task focused on just five technical features. To answer relevantly, it would have been necessary to think of examples of these features from the poem, and then organise them into a paragraph plan that would lead to a clearly structured analysis of their importance to the text.

This was a challenging task. As well as recalling the specified features in sufficient detail, a lot of self-discipline would be required by the candidate to avoid lapsing into a more general, pre-prepared commentary.

Identifying the key words

To pass the critical essay, your understanding must be shown *to be appropriate to the task set.*

This means that you must *apply* your knowledge and carry out the task exactly as it is asked in the question. If you have taken the recommended few minutes to read all the questions carefully, you should have noted what the details of the task are and assessed your fitness to answer them before making your final choice of question.

A strategy that will help you stay on task is to identify clearly the *key words* of the question. The key words are those that provide the details of the task. They will appear in both the first and second sentences of the question. It will help to underline or highlight them. You should then make sure you repeat them throughout your essay.

For example:

> Choose a play in which a character feels increasingly isolated from the community in which he or she lives.
>
> Show how the dramatist makes you aware of the character's increasing isolation and discuss how it affects your attitude to the character.

The key words of the task are 'character', 'isolated', 'increasing isolation' and 'attitude to the character'.

You could pick them out in the following way:

> Choose a play in which a <u>character</u> feels increasingly <u>isolated</u> from the community in which he or she lives.
>
> Show how the dramatist makes you aware of the character's <u>increasing isolation</u> and discuss how it affects your <u>attitude to the character</u> .

Because you will be repeating these ideas throughout your essay, it is a good idea to jot down some synonyms (words with the same meaning) for the key words which you can use to vary your language.

For example, for 'isolated' you might jot down:

Isolated:

alienated
separate
separated
set apart
insulated
cut off

For Practice 3

1   Copy out the following questions and underline or highlight the key words that define the task.

2   Make lists of synonyms that you could use for *one or more* of the key words.

   A   Choose a novel or short story in which a conflict between two of the main characters is central to the story. Explain how the conflict arises and go on to discuss in detail how the writer uses it to explore an important theme.

   B   Choose a poem in which the poet has created a perfect blend of form and content. Show how the poet achieves this and discuss how it adds to your appreciation of the poem.

   C   Choose a play in which there is a scene involving intense emotion. Show how the dramatist makes you aware of the intensity of the emotion in the scene and discuss the importance of the scene to the drama as a whole.

   D   Choose a poem in which the poet creates a picture of a heroic or a corrupt figure. Discuss the means by which the personality is clearly depicted.

   E   Choose a novel which is influenced by the presence of a powerful or overbearing character. Show how the novelist creates this impression of the character and discuss to what extent you felt you could sympathise with him or her.

   F   Choose a play in which one scene or moment determines the fate of a main character. Explain fully why you think this is the key moment in the character's fortunes.

Breaking down the task

It is essential that you focus on your task from the planning stage if you are to gain a good mark.

Having identified your key words, you should then try to break down the task into the various elements or strands of discussion that it involves.

For example, one question in the poetry section for 2006 read:

Choose a poem that deals with a childhood experience .

Discuss to what extent the poet's description of the experience leads you to a clear understanding of the poet's theme .

The highlighted words are the key words of the task. You could now bullet-point the strands you must include in your discussion if you are to fulfil the task. These could be as follows:

- Identify a childhood experience.

- Analyse how the poet describes the experience.

- Relate your understanding of the theme to the description of the experience.

Having done this, you can then relate the strands to your own text. For this question, a suitable text could be Liz Lochead's poem 'Revelation'.

The plan could be adapted to:

- *Experience*: being shown the farm's bull.

- *Description*: use of senses – colour, smell, shape, sound; contrasts with hens.

- *Relation to theme*: awareness of dark side of life, sexuality, danger leading to loss of childhood innocence.

For Practice 4

1 For each of the questions on page 38, provide a breakdown of the strands of the task in bullet points.

2 Chose one or more questions that are suitable for your own texts and write brief plans using the 'Revelation' plan as an example.

Recognising what is important

Note an important instruction that applies to *all* tasks in *all* genres:

> Answers to questions…should address relevantly the central concern(s)/theme(s) of the text.

An explanation of 'central concerns' was given on page 6. It is important to remember that your essay must show clear understanding of the *main* ideas. If you choose a question that directs you to a scene of a play or an episode of a book, you will always be expected to show how it reflects or illustrates these main ideas. This will require you to show a good overall grasp of the *whole* text.

Appropriate literary techniques

Another instruction that applies in every case is:

> Answers to questions…should…be supported by reference to appropriate techniques.

The examiner will expect you to show understanding and appreciation of various literary techniques and evaluate their importance to whichever aspect of the text is the focus of your essay.

To help you, a list of these techniques is given on the critical essay paper; it appears either at the end of the question or in a box at the top of the section.

These are *open* lists. This means that you don't need to restrict your choice to the techniques listed but you could mention others that seem relevant to your discussion.

The lists of techniques vary according to the genre, but you will notice that some are appropriate to all the genres.

Drama

In this genre, you are directed to:

> …conflict, characterisation, key scene(s), dialogue, climax, exposition, denouement, structure, plot, setting, aspects of staging (such as lighting, music, stage set, stage directions…), soliloquy, monologue…

A glossary explaining these terms is to be found on pages 129–132.

The terms in brackets referring to aspects of staging might be appropriate if your teacher has prepared you to write on an actual performance. Alternatively, you might choose them if you have studied a play that makes particular reference to them. For example, in *A Streetcar Named Desire* by Tennesee Williams, the aspects of staging listed in brackets are all very important to the understanding of the central concerns of the text.

Do not be afraid to use other techniques as you think appropriate. For example, in Arthur Miller's play *All My Sons*, symbolism is very important in the enclosed backyard setting and in the broken tree.

A scene from Arthur Miller's *All My Sons*

Prose

In the case of prose fiction, you are directed to:

> …characterisation, setting, key incident(s), narrative technique, symbolism, structure, climax, plot, atmosphere, dialogue, imagery…

In the case of prose non-fiction, you are directed to:

> …ideas, use of evidence, selection of detail, stance, setting, anecdote, narrative voice, style, language, structure, organisation of material…

A glossary explaining these terms is to be found on pages 129–132.

You should remember that these terms are suggestions only, and some of the techniques suggested for fiction might be appropriate for a non-fiction text. Non-fiction is sometimes presented using the conventions of fiction, in which case it would be acceptable to use terms like 'characterisation' and 'plot', and to refer to the book as a 'novel'. A well-known example is *Biko* by Donald Woods, which presents true events in the life of South African political activist Steve Biko in this *emotive* way.

However, in the case of non-fiction that is clearly written as such, terms such as 'plot' would not be appropriate.

Poetry

In this genre you are directed to the following:

> …imagery, verse form, structure, mood, tone, sound, rhythm, rhyme, characterisation, contrast, setting, symbolism, word choice…

A glossary explaining these terms is to be found on pages 129–132.

In this context, and in the questions on poetry, 'sound' means the sound of the words that the poet chooses, and his or her use of techniques such as alliteration, assonance and onomatopoeia.

✗ **Don't** use these terms as subheadings in your essay. The unity of your essay is important, and it should not be split into sections.

These lists of technical terms are to remind you to focus on *how* your texts are written, not just on *what* they say.

Remembering the genre

Another important point regarding the *'relevance of your essays to the questions you have chosen'* applies particularly to drama. Don't forget that even if you have read it from a book in the classroom, a play is meant to be *performed* and aims to create a response in an audience who are both watching and listening. Many candidates refer to their text as 'a book' or to 'the reader' instead of 'the audience', which shows that they have forgotten this.

The way to show your awareness of the drama genre is to refer to 'the audience' in your analysis, and refer frequently to other features that pertain to drama, such as stage directions, speeches, scenes and the stage. Remember also that although they may be realistic, the characters are not real people: try to show that they are the creations of the playwright. This means concentrating on what the characters do and say in the play, what others say about them and how they are shown interacting with others. Avoid speculating on what the characters *might* have done, or what they *think*, as if they have lives outside the drama.

For Practice 5

The following examples of drama analysis are printed in pairs. In one example of each pair there are obvious errors of approach to the genre. The other example is correct. Can you identify which example is which and why? State the example you think is wrong and write down your reasons. Pick out phrases from the other example that show good awareness of the genre.

The examples refer to Shakespeare's *Hamlet*, a play in which Hamlet, the Prince of Denmark, suspects that his uncle has murdered his father, the King. His uncle, Claudius, has married Hamlet's mother and become king.   →

1 **(a)** When we first see Hamlet in the Danish court he stands out visually because he is the only courtier wearing black. This prepares the audience for the conflict between Hamlet and Claudius, which comes into the open when Claudius complains to Hamlet that he is failing to enter into the spirit of the marriage celebrations.

   (b) Hamlet and Claudius do not get on from the start of the play. In addition to the fact that Hamlet is still mourning his father's death, Hamlet is very upset because his mother whom he loves very much has married his hated uncle. We can therefore feel sorry for Hamlet because he must feel very jealous and confused.

Example … shows errors of approach because…

_____

_____

_____

_____

_____

_____

_____

Example … shows good practice because…

_____

_____

_____

_____

_____

_____

_____

➜

2 **(a)** After Claudius and the other courtiers leave, the reader learns that Hamlet is feeling suicidal: 'O that this too, too solid flesh would melt'. He is so depressed at the way his life has turned out that he feels there is really no other solution to his problems. Only the fact that God's law forbids 'self-slaughter' stops him. The reader can understand how he feels because many young people feel lonely and cut off from adults in this way.

(b) When Hamlet is left alone on stage he delivers a moving soliloquy in which he reveals that he is contemplating suicide. The strength of his feeling as he compares his father to his uncle is powerfully communicated to the audience, whose sympathy is aroused by his bitter comment that his heart is breaking but he must nevertheless 'hold his tongue' for the present. The fact that Hamlet is alone on stage emphasises his vulnerability compared to Claudius, who exits surrounded by courtiers.

Example … shows errors of approach because…

_____

_____

_____

_____

_____

_____

_____

_____

Example … shows good practice because…

_____

_____

_____

_____

_____

_____

_____

_____

Planning the Essay

Once you have chosen a text which fits the question, and identified all the key words in order to establish exactly what the task is, you must then plan your essay.

- You will *not* be marked on your plan.
- You will *not* gain any extra credit for showing that you have made a plan.
- Don't forget to cross it out, or mark it clearly as a plan.

The advantage you gain will be that your essay will be relevant to the task and show a sustained, coherent line of thought. It is this that will gain the marks.

Watch your time! Spending five or even ten minutes thinking and planning will be invaluable. But don't let the plan take on a life of its own.

A plan should contain	A plan should not contain
✔ key words from the question	✗ question written out in full
✔ brief notes/headings	✗ complete sentences
✔ key words to remind you of quotations	✗ quotations in full
✔ abbreviations	
✔ some indication of how you will order/arrange your material	

Styles of plan

Suppose a candidate has studied the prose fiction text *Lord of the Flies* by William Golding.

(The book is about a group of young schoolboys who survive a plane crash on a desert island. There are no adults, and the boys must organise themselves. Gradually, all but a very few boys abandon the civilised behaviour they have learned and descend into savagery and murder.)

The candidate has chosen the following question from the prose fiction section:

> Choose a novel or short story in which a conflict between two of the main characters is central to the story.
>
> Explain how the conflict arises and go on to discuss in detail how the writer uses it to explore an important theme .

This question is a good 'fit' for her text.

She has highlighted the key words from the question and identified three strands of discussion that she must cover in order to fulfil the task:

- Identify a conflict between two main characters that is central to the story.

- Explain how the conflict between the characters arises.

- Explain how an important theme is explored through this conflict.

She has decided to choose the conflict between Ralph and Jack to illustrate the theme of good and evil in human nature. She adapts her text to the strands of the task:

- Jack and Ralph are two main characters who are in conflict.

- Conflict arises due to jealousy, and their conflicting attitudes and aims.

- The theme of good and evil in human nature is explored, with Jack's side representing negative aspects and Ralph's representing positive aspects.

She organises her ideas into three boxes:

Characters of Jack and Ralph	Conflict arises	Themes explored
Situation: war in adult world forms backdrop to their conflict. Isolation of island and lack of adults throws responsibilities onto boys.	Boys choose Ralph as leader; Jack is disappointed and jealous. Jack's jealousy leads him to create breakaway group with different aims to Ralph's: hunting and 'fun'.	Different aspects of human nature – opposing impulses to savagery and civilisation. Book written in wake of discovery of Second World War atrocities and author's teaching experience of schoolboys' bullying and cruelty.

Characters of Jack and Ralph	Conflict arises	Characters of Jack and Ralph
Contrast between Ralph, 'the fair boy' / 'something dark': Jack is associated with red (hair) and black (cloak and cap), colours of Nazis.	Ralph supports use of conch, symbol of democracy; Jack becomes a dictator and is ultimately responsible for smashing the conch.	Ralph stands for civilised values against Jack's enjoyment of cruelty and reversion to savagery with his 'tribe', war paint and hunting.
Some similarities: Ralph likes fun, like Jack is strong and athletic – swims well and stands on his head; not specially clever.	Ralph has responsible ideas: to build shelters, keep a fire alight and attract rescue; Jack is too impatient to help.	Jack appeals to other boys on primitive level – provides meat and dancing; exploits their fears. This explains how he influences others.
Ralph values Piggy for common sense and wisdom; Jack despises Piggy for physical weakness.	Jack also wants fire to cook and must physically fight for Piggy's glasses, which can make fire.	Ralph offers routine drudgery of hard work and obeying rules, which has long-term but not short-term gratification.
Pig-killing episode illustrates that Ralph also has impulses to kill, but he will exercise self-control.	Ralph shows moral awareness over death of Simon; Jack is unrepentant.	Fire and destruction caused by Jack and his tribe at the end mirror destruction of the Second World War. Ralph is almost annihilated like victims of war.

The candidate might jot down at the same time some notes for quotations she could use in evidence. She could attach these to the margins of the boxes.

A spider plan

A popular style of plan is the 'spider' diagram. Here is an example based on a question from the 2005 drama paper, using Shakespeare's *Macbeth* as the text. The question and notes are entered in more detail than you need to do on your own plans so that you can understand them.

> Choose a play in which the mood is mainly dark or pessimistic .
>
> Show how the dramatist creates this mood and discuss how appropriate it is to the main idea(s) of the play.

Strands of task:

- Identify dark, pessimistic mood in play.

- Explain how dramatist creates this sense of darkness/pessimism.

- Explain how main ideas fit into mood appropriately.

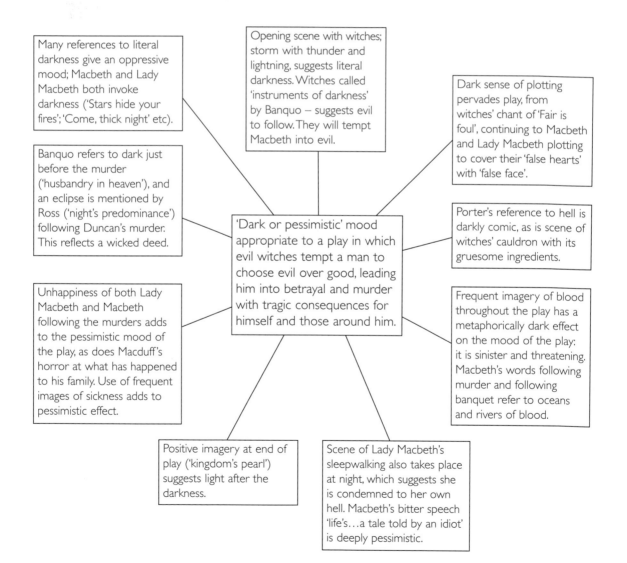

Many references to literal darkness give an oppressive mood; Macbeth and Lady Macbeth both invoke darkness ('Stars hide your fires'; 'Come, thick night' etc).

Opening scene with witches; storm with thunder and lightning, suggests literal darkness. Witches called 'instruments of darkness' by Banquo – suggests evil to follow. They will tempt Macbeth into evil.

Dark sense of plotting pervades play, from witches' chant of 'Fair is foul', continuing to Macbeth and Lady Macbeth plotting to cover their 'false hearts' with 'false face'.

Banquo refers to dark just before the murder ('husbandry in heaven'), and an eclipse is mentioned by Ross ('night's predominance') following Duncan's murder. This reflects a wicked deed.

'Dark or pessimistic' mood appropriate to a play in which evil witches tempt a man to choose evil over good, leading him into betrayal and murder with tragic consequences for himself and those around him.

Porter's reference to hell is darkly comic, as is scene of witches' cauldron with its gruesome ingredients.

Unhappiness of both Lady Macbeth and Macbeth following the murders adds to the pessimistic mood of the play, as does Macduff's horror at what has happened to his family. Use of frequent images of sickness adds to pessimistic effect.

Frequent imagery of blood throughout the play has a metaphorically dark effect on the mood of the play: it is sinister and threatening. Macbeth's words following murder and following banquet refer to oceans and rivers of blood.

Positive imagery at end of play ('kingdom's pearl') suggests light after the darkness.

Scene of Lady Macbeth's sleepwalking also takes place at night, which suggests she is condemned to her own hell. Macbeth's bitter speech 'life's…a tale told by an idiot' is deeply pessimistic.

A good way to test how comprehensive your preparation has been is to prepare plans for as many questions as possible. Note that this exercise involves writing plans only – not the actual essays.

For Practice 6

1   Prepare a number of plans for questions from past papers using your own texts. You could choose the 'spider' format, as in the *Macbeth* example, or the box format, as in the *Lord of the Flies* example.

2   Practise writing plans against the clock. Stop after ten minutes and see how useful a plan you have achieved.

3   Compile a list of useful abbreviations that you can use for your own texts.

While you might show the plans to your teacher, who can advise you if you seem to be on the right track, do not write the whole essays and do not be overly concerned about getting marks.

Shaping your essay

A good plan can help you shape your essay. By arranging your material beforehand you can avoid several of the common pitfalls:

✗   Retelling the story.

✗   Having a bad balance, for example by spending too much time on the first half of a text.

✗   Ordering your material in a confused manner.

✗   Omitting parts of the task.

Writing the Introductory Paragraph

The actor and politician Arnold Schwarzenegger, a former bodybuilder and holder of the 'Mr Universe' title, once offered the following advice: 'Start wide, expand further, and never look back'.

That might be a good suggestion to follow in many areas of life, but it's not much help when it comes to writing an essay!

What you should not do

The opening paragraph of an essay should *not* take a wide, general approach but should focus directly on the question.

✗ **Don't** start by talking about the life and background of the author.

✗ **Don't** begin by giving a detailed account of the plot.

✗ **Don't** go into detailed discussion about characters, themes, etc.

✗ **Don't** include quotations or examples.

✗ **Don't** try to be amusing or dramatic. (This is fine in creative writing, but not in a literature essay.)

The 'five-step' formula

Even if you find essay-writing difficult, you should be able to get your answer off to a good start by following a simple five-step formula:

> 1 Identify the text and author.
>
> 2 Use words from the beginning of the question and explain why the chosen text is suitable for the question.
>
> 3 Include a sentence or two summarising the text (but no more than a sentence or two).
>
> 4 Refer to the words that set the task in the second sentence of the question.
>
> 5 Give an idea of how the rest of the essay is going to develop in order to fulfil the task.

Imagine that you are writing an essay in answer to the following question:

> Choose a poem in which a specific setting is strongly evoked.
>
> Show how the poet creates this sense of place and/or time, and then discuss the relative importance of the setting to the poem as a whole.

Remember that the poetry section of the Higher question paper also contains the following instructions:

> Answers to questions on poetry should address relevantly the central concern(s)/theme(s) of the text(s) and be supported by reference to appropriate poetic techniques such as: imagery, verse form, structure, mood, tone, sound, rhythm, rhyme, characterisation, contrast, setting, symbolism, word choice…

A poem that would fit this question well is 'Brooklyn Cop' by Norman MacCaig.

Brooklyn Cop

Built like a gorilla but less timid,
thick-fleshed, steak-coloured, with two
hieroglyphs in his face that mean
trouble, he walks the sidewalk and the
thin tissue over violence. This morning
when he said, 'See you, babe' to his wife,
he hoped it, he truly hoped it.
He is a gorilla to whom 'Hiya, honey' is no cliché.

Should the tissue tear, should he plunge through
into violence, what clubbings, what
gunshots between Phoebe's
Whamburger and Louie's Place.

Who would be him, gorilla with a nightstick,
whose home is a place
he might, this time, never get back to?

And who would be who have to be
his victims?

In your study of the poem you are likely to cover points such as these:

- The poem depicts the violent atmosphere of this part of New York – that is, a specific setting is strongly evoked.

- Much of the poem is devoted to a description of the 'cop', whose appearance and character have been shaped by his violent surroundings.

- The poet conveys this through the use of similes and metaphors (imagery).

Here is how these points could be fitted into an opening paragraph:

Name of text and author	A poem that strongly evokes a specific setting is 'Brooklyn Cop' by Norman MacCaig. The poet describes the dangers	*Reference to words of the question*
Brief summary of the poem	faced by a New York policeman on a day-to-day basis and shows that he has had to develop a toughness and brutality in order	
Refers to words from the question that set the task (namely setting and its importance to the poem as a whole)	to survive in this place. A strong impression of the violent atmosphere in the Brooklyn area is conveyed, which is of paramount importance in portraying the policeman. By establishing the setting through the use of vivid imagery and word choice, MacCaig makes it clear that the policeman's personality and physical appearance have been shaped by the violence surrounding him.	*The last sentence makes it clear that key aspects such as 'setting' and 'imagery' mentioned in the question will be examined in more detail in the rest of the essay*

For Discussion

The same basic structure can be used to write an introductory paragraph in any genre. For Practice 7 shows some introductions written by Higher English candidates in response to the following question from the drama section:

> Choose a play which you feel has a memorable opening section.
>
> Show how the content or the atmosphere of the scene or section provides an effective starting point for the development of the characters and the theme of the play.

Remember that the drama section of the Higher question paper also contains the following instructions:

> Answers to questions on drama should address relevantly the central concern(s)/theme(s) of the text(s) and be supported by reference to appropriate dramatic techniques such as: conflict, characterisation, key scene(s), dialogue, climax, exposition, denouement, structure, plot, setting, aspects of staging, soliloquy, monologue…

For Practice 7

In pairs or groups, discuss how effective each of the following seven examples would be as the opening paragraph for an essay in response to the question above.

Put a tick or a cross in the box according to whether each of the five steps outlined on page 50 have been carried out.

Tip!

The introductory paragraph should be so closely related to the words of the question that you should be able to work out what the question is even if you don't have it in front of you.

If you can't do this, the introduction is not clear enough!

Bear this in mind when discussing these seven sample introductions.

(You do not need to be familiar with *Romeo and Juliet* or *Macbeth* to complete this task.)

A   A play that has a memorable opening section is *Romeo and Juliet*. The memorable opening section is the prologue. The prologue tells the reader of the outcome of the play in advance. This provides an effective starting point for the development of the characters and the theme of the play.

1	
2	
3	
4	
5	

→

B A play that has a memorable opening section is *Romeo and Juliet* by William Shakespeare. The opening section takes the form of a prologue, which summarises the whole play by telling the audience that it traces the story of two young lovers, Romeo and Juliet, who belong to opposing families, the Montagues and Capulets, who are locked in a bitter feud in the medieval Italian city of Verona. By announcing in advance that the play will end with the death of the lovers, the prologue introduces the theme of fate that determines the development of the tragedy.

1	
2	
3	
4	
5	

C *Romeo and Juliet* is a tragic love story about two young lovers who lived in Verona in Italy in the Middle Ages. Romeo belongs to the Montague family while Juliet is a Capulet and their parents would not allow them to associate with each other because the families are bitter enemies. The opening of the play is memorable because there is a fight. The feud between the families has lasted for centuries. One member of the Capulet family, Tybalt, wants to keep the feud going but Romeo is not interested because he is in love with Juliet. One of the turning points in the play is in Act 3 where Romeo is drawn into a fight against his will and kills Tybalt. This is also a memorable part of the play.

1	
2	
3	
4	
5	

D *Romeo and Juliet* by William Shakespeare tells the story of a feud between two families, the Montagues and the Capulets. However, some of the Montagues gatecrash a party at the Capulets' house and there Romeo falls in love with Juliet. They fall in love immediately but keep this secret because their parents disapprove. Fights between the two opposing families are constantly breaking out and Romeo kills Tybalt, leading to him being banished from Verona as a punishment. The two lovers were secretly married by Friar Lawrence and they turn to him for help. He gives Juliet a special drug that makes it look as if she has died but Romeo arrives before she wakes up and kills himself because he thinks she is dead. She then wakes up and commits suicide too.

1	
2	
3	
4	
5	

E *Macbeth* has a memorable opening because he meets the witches. He is a very ambitious man and his wife persuades him to kill King Duncan and make himself king. However, he feels guilty about this and his conscience troubles him: 'Macbeth shall sleep no more'. Later he hires murderers to kill his friend Banquo and, towards the end of the play, has Macduff's family killed too. At the end of the story King Duncan's son Malcolm becomes king. The play was written by William Shakespeare.

1	
2	
3	
4	
5	

→

F After seeing the film of *Romeo and Juliet* starring Leonardo di Caprio and Claire Danes I couldn't wait to read the play itself. *Romeo and Juliet* is one of the world's most romantic love stories. Although Shakespeare wrote it in the sixteenth century it can still be enjoyed by an audience today.

1	
2	
3	
4	
5	

G A play that has a memorable opening is William Shakespeare's *Macbeth*. By introducing the audience to three witches, the first scene immediately establishes an atmosphere of evil, confusion and mystery. The fact that the witches mention Macbeth already implies that they will have some connection with this character and foreshadows the development of evil within him that is a key theme of the play.

1	
2	
3	
4	
5	

Thinking it over

When you have discussed each of these introductory paragraphs in your group, summarise your findings in a table as follows.

	Strengths	Weaknesses
A.		
B.		
C.		
D.		
E.		
F.		
G.		

Which was the best introduction? Which was the weakest?

Did everyone in the class agree?

For Practice 8

Look at the following critical essay question on poetry:

> Choose a poem in which the writer's use of poetic techniques plays an important part.
>
> Show how these techniques play a significant role in helping you to understand the subject matter of the poem.

Remember that the poetry section of the Higher question paper also contains the following instructions:

> Answers to questions on poetry should address relevantly the central concern(s)/ theme(s) of the text(s) and be supported by reference to appropriate poetic techniques such as: imagery, verse form, structure, mood, tone, sound, rhythm, rhyme, characterisation, contrast, setting, symbolism, word choice...

Using *either* the material on 'Brooklyn Cop' covered on pages 51–52 *or* another poem you have been studying in class, write an introductory paragraph for an essay answering this question.

Exchange answers with a partner and decide whether your introduction covers the five points listed on page 50.

Developing the Essay

Plot summary: is it needed?

There's no doubt that the introduction is the most important paragraph in any essay and, if you follow the suggestions in the previous section, you should always be able to get your essay off to a good start.

Of course, the rest of the essay must then go on to do what was promised in the introduction!

You might be tempted to write a paragraph summarising the story but it is generally not a good idea to do this.

One point that is emphasised throughout this book is that a critical essay is always an answer to a specific question, and never a general summary of the book, play or poem.

If paragraph two of your essay starts retelling the story, there's a danger that the essay will just continue in this way and forget the question.

Nevertheless, it would be equally wrong if the essay did not provide any background about the plot at all. There has to be some kind of context: don't just assume that the reader knows what you are referring to.

Putting things in context

Here's an extract from an essay on *Lord of the Flies* by William Golding. This is the second paragraph and follows on from the introduction:

```
At the start of the story Piggy is delighted to be free of adult control.
'The delight of a realised ambition overcame him.' He finds a conch and
when he discovers it can make a noise he suggests to Ralph that they could
use it to call the others together to discuss the situation they are in.
```

The problem here is that the writer just assumes we know the background. There are too many unanswered questions.

> | *How has this* | At the start of the story *Piggy* is | *Who?* |
> | --- | --- | --- |
> | *happened?* | delighted to be *free of adult control*. | |
> | | 'The delight of a realised ambition | |
> | *What?* | overcame him.' He finds a *conch* and when | |
> | | he discovers it can make a noise he | |
> | | suggests to *Ralph* that they could use it | *Who?* |
> | *Who?* | to call *the others* together to discuss *the* | |
> | | *situation* they are in. | *What situation?* |

Here is someone else's attempt to write that paragraph:

> The story begins with a group of boys who have survived an air crash on a tropical island. Piggy, an overweight boy who suffers from asthma and wears glasses, is delighted by the 'realised ambition' of being freed from adult control. He finds a large shell, known as a conch, and when he discovers it can make a noise he suggests to another boy, Ralph, that they could use it to round up the other boys to discuss how best to survive in this new and unfamiliar environment.

For Discussion

Why is this better than the first version?

Remember

- When a character is mentioned for the first time, he or she should be introduced briefly.

- In the same way, the setting of the story should be explained, if this is relevant.

- If an event is mentioned, it should be placed in context – for example where does it fit into the sequence of events?

Tip!

The paragraph should make sense to a reader who has never read the book.

For Practice 9

1 Here is some material summarising part of Robin Jenkins' novel *The Changeling*.

On the left hand side is a very brief summary, which does not place characters or events in context. On the right hand side is some fuller background information.

Combine material from both sources to create an improved summary paragraph that would make sense to someone who had not read the book.

Outline summary	Background on characters and settings
Tom Curdie lives in Donaldson's Court and has a difficult family background. Charlie Forbes decides to take Tom to Towellan, but he is mocked by his colleague Todd for doing this. Mary needs to be persuaded before she agrees to the plan, because she is worried about the effect it will have on Gillian and Alistair.	*Charlie Forbes:* a school teacher who feels that it is his duty not only to teach his classes but to care for pupils who have difficult lives and to try to help them.
	Tom Curdie: a neglected and undernourished boy whose intelligence is being channelled into dishonest activities.
	Donaldson's Court: a notorious slum area.
	Towellan: a holiday town on the Clyde Coast where the Forbes family have the use of a cottage each summer.
	Mr Todd: the Depute Head at the school where Forbes teaches. He is cynical about Forbes, seeing him as a 'do-gooder'.
	Mary: Charlie Forbes' wife, who takes a common-sense and realistic approach to life.
	Gillian and Alistair: children in the Forbes family.

> **Tip!**
>
> If you write a brief account, make sure it is brief!
>
> Two ways of keeping it brief:
>
> 1 Simply summarise what happens. Don't start saying why it was a memorable scene, or why it was important for the rest of the play: these are the topics to be discussed later in the essay.
>
> 2 Quotations will probably not be necessary in this part of the essay. Again, keep them for later on.

2 Earlier, we looked at how to write an introductory paragraph for a question on a play with a memorable opening section (page 52).

This is the type of question where it *would* be a good idea to write a short account of the scene in the second paragraph of the essay. It would be necessary to explain *what* happens in the scene before you could go on to show *why* it was memorable.

If you have been studying a play in class, write a single paragraph outlining what happens in the opening scene or act.

One step at a time

The previous section looked at the pros and cons of following the introductory paragraph with a short outline of the book, chapter or scene.

If you decide that it's appropriate to do this, remember to keep the outline short, providing only the background information that will be needed to understand the main argument of the essay.

In the remainder of the essay, you should pick up on the points mentioned in your introduction and expand on these in detail.

If you have studied your text, made detailed notes and compiled a bank of quotations (as discussed in Part 1 of this book), you will have plenty of material to draw on.

It's not enough to simply learn all of your notes before the exam. Pouring out all your material in one go will not produce a good essay! It must be properly structured, presenting points in a *step-by-step* fashion.

> 99
>
> 'If you're climbing the ladder of life, you go rung by rung, one step at a time. Don't look too far up; set your goals high but take one step at a time.'
>
> *(Donny Osmond, musician)*

The pattern should be

- make one point

- back it up with evidence

- *link* to the next point

- back this one up with evidence, and so on.

Structuring paragraphs properly

You will probably have heard the term *topic sentence* before. This refers to one sentence (usually the first one in the paragraph) that sums up what the rest of the paragraph is going to deal with.

- A topic sentence will make a general point, not a detailed one.

- It should refer to words from the question.

Look at these two sentences:

> The opening scene of *Romeo and Juliet* is a memorable one for several reasons.

> When Romeo and his friends gatecrash a party at the Capulets' house, Romeo falls in love with Juliet.

The first one is a topic sentence but the second one is not.

The first example leads us to expect that the rest of the paragraph will explain the reasons why the scene is memorable; the second example simply tells us part of the story. It gives no indication about what will come next.

Think of the topic sentence as a signpost. It indicates the direction in which the rest of the paragraph is going to travel.

For Practice 10

Discuss how effective each of the following would be as a topic sentence at the start of a paragraph:

Sentence	What clues are given about how the rest of the paragraph is likely to develop?
1 *Romeo* and *Juliet* is a tragic love story about two young lovers who lived in Verona in Italy in the Middle Ages.	
2 The prologue to *Romeo* and *Juliet* introduces the theme of fate.	
3 Shortly after this, Duncan came to visit Macbeth at his castle because he was very pleased at how well Macbeth fought in the battle.	
4 'Trailed his slackness soft-bellied down.' Here the poet is effectively describing how the snake slithers down and uses alliteration of the 's' sounds.	
5 The poet's use of imagery creates a strong impression of the violent atmosphere on the streets of Brooklyn.	
6 Lady Macbeth uses several different methods to put pressure on her husband to murder King Duncan.	
7 In Act 1 Scene 3 the witches prophesy that Macbeth will become king of Scotland.	

➜

9 Charlie Forbes decides to take Tom to Towellan, but he is mocked by his colleague Todd for doing this.	
10 The opening scene of *Macbeth* establishes an atmosphere of mystery and evil, which is developed in the rest of the play.	
11 The author's use of symbolism helps the reader to understand the development of the character of Tom Curdie.	
12 'The delight of a realised ambition overcame him.' This shows that Piggy is delighted to be free of adult control.	

Proving your points with evidence

One of the golden rules of writing a critical essay is that *a statement must be backed up with evidence.*

'Evidence' might be:

- A *direct* quotation (such as the actual words said by a character in a play).
- An *indirect* reference to something that happens in the text. (For example, a sentence summarising Piggy's suggestion about using the conch to call a meeting could be used as evidence that he is a character who comes up with practical ideas.)

Using quotations convincingly

Simply learning up quotations and reproducing them will not make a good essay.

When a quotation is used as evidence, it must be put in context: introduce it properly by making it clear who spoke these words, where they came into the story, and so on.

For example:

'We've got to decide if this is an island.' Ralph takes command and tells the others what to do.	✘ Don't begin the paragraph with a quotation. There should always be a statement first.
In *Lord of the Flies*, Ralph is a character who exhibits strong qualities of leadership. 'We've got to decide if this is an island.'	✘ Statement is followed by a quotation, but it is not clear who said these words, or when.
In *Lord of the Flies*, Ralph is a character who exhibits strong qualities of leadership. For example, at the first meeting of the survivors it is he who stresses to the others that 'We've got to decide if this is an island.'	✔ Statement is followed by a quotation that is placed in a context.

Here's a useful 'formula' to follow when writing a paragraph unit in a critical essay:

Critical essay paragraph unit

1   Make a general statement (topic sentence).

2   Find a quotation that backs it up.

3   Introduce the quotation by placing it in context. (For example, who says it? At what stage of the story does it come?)

4   Follow the quotation with a comment. (For example what does it show about the character/theme/setting?) In a poetry essay, the comment might analyse the poet's word choice, imagery or other techniques.

The following is an example of a typical paragraph from an essay on *Macbeth*. The comments in the right-hand column explain what each sentence is trying to do.

Topic sentence *Context*	In the first act of the play, Macbeth is a highly regarded figure in Scotland. He has shown his bravery and loyalty by winning the battle against the invading Norwegian army, which had been assisted by a traitor, the Thane of Cawdor, and is described by the Captain as	*Statement about Macbeth's reputation* *Summary of events in the plot that reveal qualities of his character*
Quotations	'brave Macbeth – well he deserves that name –	*Quotation giving evidence to show that others respect Macbeth*
Comment	Disdaining fortune, with his brandish'd steel'	
	The choice of the word 'disdaining', which means to regard with contempt, emphasises how fearless Macbeth is on the battlefield.	*Comment on writer's technique (in this case, the effectiveness of the word choice)*
Linking expression leads into next point	In the same way, one of the Scottish noblemen, Ross, calls Macbeth 'Bellona's bridegroom'. This reference to the Roman goddess of war also stresses Macbeth's skill and courage on the battlefield.	*Second piece of evidence makes the argument more convincing* *Comment summarises what the evidence shows about Macbeth's character and reputation*

Tip!

Structure your paragraphs on this pattern:

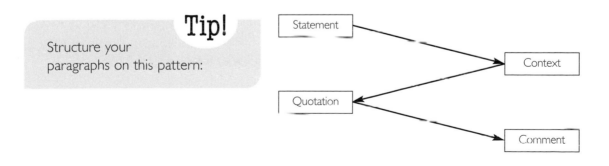

For Practice 11

Using any poem you have studied in class, write a practice paragraph based on the following structure:

Opening words	What you should do
First sentence: One technique that the poet uses effectively is…	Pick any technique used by the poet such as imagery, word choice, irony, rhyme, alliteration, etc.
Second sentence: For example…	Introduce a quotation by placing it in context and explaining any background information necessary to understand the example to be given.
Third sentence: [Quote directly from the poem.]	Select one or two lines that illustrate the technique mentioned in the first sentence.
Fourth sentence: This is effective because…	Comment on how the quotation increases your understanding of the subject of the poem. If you have chosen an image (such as a simile or metaphor), you should • identify what is compared to what • explain what the two have in common.

For Practice 12

Look at the following paragraphs from essays written by candidates studying Higher English.

In pairs or groups, discuss the questions in the right-hand column, which will help you decide how well-structured these paragraphs are and how effectively they use quotations as back-up evidence.

I   In 'Brooklyn Cop', MacCaig's word choice and use of imagery create a picture of a violent society. The area that the policeman controls is an inner-city part of New York where brutality and bloodshed are everyday occurrences. The poet describes how the officer

> 'walks the sidewalk and the thin tissue over
> violence.'

A 'thin tissue' is obviously a very fragile and easily removed covering; in the same way, the veneer of civilisation is completely powerless to suppress the violence that erupts in the streets on a daily basis. The speed at which this can happen is emphasised in the second verse, which considers what could happen

> 'should the tissue tear, should he plunge through
> into violence.'

The word ' plunge' implies a sudden and brutal immersion in the violent atmosphere.

What role does the opening sentence play in the paragraph?

What is the purpose of the second sentence?

How is this quotation connected to the previous sentence?

How does the sentence add to your understanding of the quotation above?

Why is a second quotation included here?

Brooklyn apartment blocks

2   The prologue of *Romeo and Juliet* provides an effective starting point for the theme of fate. It does this by telling the reader what is going to happen:

> 'Doth with their death bury their parents' strife.'

This quote tells the reader that they die and end the strife.

What does the opening sentence reveal about the purpose of this paragraph?

How successfully does the candidate develop this statement in the rest of the paragraph?

Suggest how the paragraph could be improved.

3   Charlie Forbes decides to take Tom Curdie on holiday to Towellan along with Mrs Forbes, Alistair and Gillian. Forbes finds it difficult to understand the boy because he gives no clue to his feelings. 'Why no laughter, no smile even, no grimace of amusement, only this intensive antagonistic contemplativeness?' Forbes asks him: 'Why in heaven's name didn't you laugh?' 'But you must learn to laugh. I don't think, Tom, I've ever heard you laugh.'

How successful is the opening as a topic sentence for the paragraph?

How effectively does the candidate use quotations?

4   Charlie Forbes acts from the best of motives towards Tom Curdie but does not fully understand the conflict within him. Tom is enjoying being at Towellan: for the first time in his life, his heart 'was beginning to thaw' and he begins to like Forbes, whom he had previously despised. At the same time, though, 'he had to remember that he would have to go back to Donaldson's Court' and that he would no longer be able to survive there 'if he went back with his heart thawed by too much love for these people'.

What two aspects of the relationship between Forbes and Tom Curdie are mentioned in the first sentence?

Show how the rest of the paragraph expands on this sentence.

→

5 Piggy is seen as being an outsider who is different from the other boys. His father is dead and his mother seems to have abandoned him to an aunt to look after. 'My auntie told me not to run on account of my asthma.' She owns a sweet shop and he is overweight. 'I used to get ever so many sweets. As many as I liked.' 'I don't care what they call me so long as they don't call me what they used to call me at school…They used to call me Piggy.' He envies Ralph for his swimming skill – 'You can't half swim well' – and says 'I can't swim. I wasn't allowed. My asthma –'

What does the opening sentence reveal about the purpose of this paragraph?

How well does the candidate provide a context for the idea that Piggy is an 'outsider'?

How effectively has the candidate used quotations?

For Practice 13

Here are a number of statements and quotations from the poem 'Brooklyn Cop'. Reorganise them into a properly constructed paragraph along the lines of the formula explained on page 64. (You are free to change the wording of the sentences – some of them repeat the same words.)

Tip!

First, decide which sentence would work best as the topic sentence and start the paragraph with this one.

The reader pictures the 'cop' as a large, tough and powerfully built individual.

The appearance of the policeman stresses how tough and violent he can be.

'built like a gorilla but less timid'

The poet uses a simile to describe the cop.

The poet is using hyperbole here to emphasise how tough and imposing the appearance of the policeman is.

The appearance and character of the Brooklyn 'cop' is entirely shaped by the environment he works in daily.

A gorilla is not a timid creature.

The poet uses a comparison to describe the police officer.

'steak-coloured'

'Steak-coloured' has connotations of something raw, tough and animal-like.

While he might not come across as a likeable figure, the 'cop' has to be the way he is in order to survive in such a hostile and aggressive environment.

For Practice 14

Now apply these skills to *any* text you have been studying in class.

- Write a clear topic sentence making a general statement.

- Develop this into a detailed paragraph.

- Use quotations.

- Put them in context.

- Comment on them in detail.

Tip!

The 'so what?' test

Don't include quotations for their own sake. For each quotation you use, ask yourself 'so what?'

If the quotation doesn't tell you anything about character, theme, etc. is it worth including it?

The Bigger Picture: Giving the Essay a Structure

So far, we have looked at how individual paragraphs should be constructed. The 'topic sentence – evidence – comment' pattern should be repeated in each paragraph in the main body of the essay.

But it is also important to keep the bigger picture in mind: what is the essay like *as a whole?*

- Is it constructed logically – in other words, does one point lead into the next that in turn leads into the next one, and so on, until a conclusion is reached?

- The essay may start off being relevant to the question but does it continue in this way?

- Are your points properly linked together? Or are they simply listed one after another?

The rest of this section gives more detailed advice on how to do this.

(Pages 13–14 showed you how to prepare 'mini' essays on selected topics from a text. These can be reused in the final, full-length essay.)

Problem	Solution
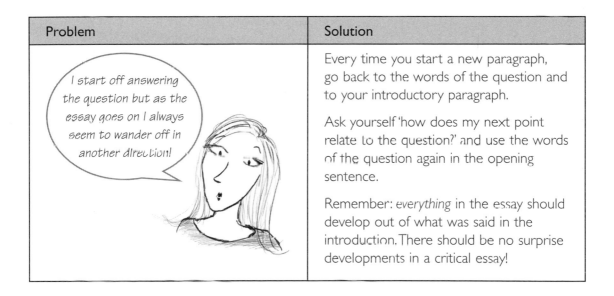 *I start off answering the question but as the essay goes on I always seem to wander off in another direction!*	Every time you start a new paragraph, go back to the words of the question and to your introductory paragraph. Ask yourself 'how does my next point relate to the question?' and use the words of the question again in the opening sentence. Remember: *everything* in the essay should develop out of what was said in the introduction. There should be no surprise developments in a critical essay!

Problem	Solution
I can think of good points to make about the text but I never seem to put them in the right order!	*Planning* is essential here. Even in an exam, you should spend a few minutes making a list of the main things you want to say. Then, use arrows or numbers to put them in the right order. Alternatively, draw a spider or box diagram (see page 48). *Before* you start writing the essay, you should be clear about the order in which you want to present your points. Otherwise, halfway through you'll probably think 'I ought to have mentioned this earlier on'.

Problem	Solution
Yes, but how do I work out what 'the right order' is?	Again, the order of your points should be determined by what you said in the introduction. Pick up each point one by one. In general, begin at the beginning of the text: don't discuss something that happens at the end and then recap to the start. Group everything about one topic in one place. For example, if you are discussing (a) development of one character, (b) setting and (c) theme, try to keep all your comments on each topic together rather than jumping from one to the other and back.

Problem	Solution
My teacher always says my essays just ramble on and on! I keep forgetting to start a new paragraph!	Very long paragraphs are a sign that the candidate is not looking back to the question. Separate what you want to say into manageable stages and deal with each one in turn. Develop one main point in a paragraph then start a new one.
	And make sure you don't end up retelling the plot! If you find your essay developing in this way *stop*, look back at the introduction and question and get back on track as soon as possible.

Paragraph plan for a critical essay

'If you don't know where you are going, you will probably end up somewhere else.'

(Laurence Peter, Canadian academic, 1919–1990)

Paragraph one: introduction

Use the words of the question and identify several points/topics that will be developed in the rest of the essay. The direction of the whole essay should be clear from the introduction onwards.

(Where appropriate, this may be followed by a paragraph giving a *brief* outline of what the text is about, especially in a 'choose a scene/chapter' type of question.)

Paragraph two

Start with a topic sentence that picks up one of the points mentioned in the introduction and develop it using the 'statement – evidence – comment' pattern. There may be several points and several quotations, but they must all develop logically from the opening topic sentence.

Paragraph three/four/five onwards

Paragraphs should develop in a similar pattern, starting with a topic sentence that returns to the introduction and picks up and develops a new point.

Conclusion

The final paragraph should sum up each of the main points that have been covered in the essay and restate your answer to the question.

This outline is shown in the following diagram:

Tip!

The most important point to remember is: stick to the question. Keep coming back to the question throughout the essay.

Paragraph One: Introduction
- Use words of question
- Identify main points of text to be discussed in the rest of the essay

---

Paragraph Two
- Topic sentence picking up a point from the introduction
- Introduction of quotation by placing it in context
- Quotation
- Detailed commentary on the significance of the quotation
- Possibly a second example/quotation
- Detailed commentary on the significance of the quotation

Paragraph Three
- Topic sentence, picking up another point from the introduction
- Use of a linking word or phrase to show how this point develops out of the previous one (see page 76 for how to do this)
- Introduction of quotation by placing it in context
- Quotation
- Detailed commentary on the significance of the quotation
- Possibly a second example/quotation
- Detailed commentary on the significance of the quotation

Paragraph Four/Five/Six
onwards should develop in a similar way, each one taking the argument forward step by step

---

Conclusion
Summing up the main points and referring back to the question

Building bridges: leading from one paragraph to the next

We have seen that a *topic sentence* makes a general statement that is developed in greater detail in the rest of the paragraph.

Another important type of sentence for essay writing is the linking sentence that forms a 'bridge' from one paragraph to the next.

A bridge must be joined at both ends! In the same way, a linking or bridging sentence picks up what was said in the previous paragraph and introduces what will be discussed in the next one.

From paragraph three onwards of your essay, you should aim to begin each paragraph with a sentence that is both a *linking* and a *topic* sentence.

For Example 1

This sentence comes from an essay on the problems faced by Tom Curdie in *The Changeling*:

'In addition to' is a linking phrase, indicating that a second point is to follow

The 'depressing physical surroundings' have been examined in the previous paragraph

In addition to his depressing physical surroundings, Tom Curdie's family background contributes to his difficulties.

How Tom's 'family background contributes to his difficulties' will be the topic of the paragraph that follows

←

Pointing back to previous paragraph

Linking sentence

→

Pointing forward to next paragraph

For Example 2

This sentence comes from an essay on the character of Charlie Forbes in *The Changeling*:

'Although' is a conjunction, indicating that the point to follow contrasts with the previous one. The positive idea ('best of intentions') contrasts with the negative one ('hostility').

'This proposal' refers back to what was discussed in the previous paragraph

Although this proposal to take Tom Curdie on the family holiday is made with the best of intentions, it is met with hostility from Charlie's work colleagues and from his wife.

The hostility of Charlie's colleagues and wife will be the topic of the paragraph that follows

←

Pointing back to previous paragraph

Linking sentence

→

Pointing forward to next paragraph

The pattern of these sentences is

1 linking expression at the start of the sentence

2 reference *back* to topic of previous paragraph

3 reference *forwards* to topic of next paragraph.

Linking expressions

There are some useful linking words and phrases that can be used to open this kind of sentence:

Adding on a similar point to the previous one:

in addition to
moreover
furthermore
in the same way
similarly

Making a different point from the previous one:

however
nevertheless
on the other hand
in contrast

Putting points in order of importance:

more significantly
of greatest importance
the most significant factor in…is…
above all

Drawing a conclusion:

therefore
consequently
as a result of this
thus

Warning!

Note that these linking words and phrases are to be used *at the start of a new sentence*. They are not *conjunctions* (e.g. and, but, when, because), which are used to join two sentences into one.

Using the linking words and phrases in the boxes above to join two sentences together would create a punctuation error. What is wrong with the following sentence?

Charlie Forbes decides to take Tom Curdie on the family holiday, however his wife is less enthusiastic.

(See pages 93–96 for more help with punctuation.)

For Practice 15

Each of the following sentences has been used by Higher English candidates as the opening to a paragraph somewhere in the middle of their essays.

Discuss how effective these sentences are as *links* in the development of the argument of the essay. How clearly does the sentence point back to what has been discussed and point forward to what comes next?

Does the sentence point back to the topic of the previous paragraph?

If so, which part of the sentence makes this clear?

Does the sentence point forward to the topic of the next paragraph?

If so, which part of the sentence makes this clear?

1 The poet's use of descriptive language not only gives the reader an idea of the violence on the streets of Brooklyn but also helps to create an impression of the character of the 'Brooklyn Cop'.

2 The use of exaggeration gives a humorous effect to some sections of the poem.

3 Thus, through using imagery and word choice, the poet succeeds in giving a detailed description of the 'Brooklyn Cop'.

4 The opening chapters of the novel introduce the reader to the theme of the effect of environment on the development of a child's character.

5 Nevertheless, Lady Macbeth's persuasion is not the only factor that leads Macbeth to murder King Duncan.

6 In contrast to Macbeth, Banquo realises that it would be unwise to trust what the witches said.

7 However, the most significant factor in Macbeth's decision to kill Duncan is not the influence of his wife or the prophecies of the witches, but his own ambition.

8 Macbeth is unable to sleep after he has killed the king because he is tormented by guilt.

9 After murdering Duncan, Macbeth returns to his wife, still with the blood-stained daggers in his hands.

10 This decision to go back to see the witches for a second time accelerates the decline of Macbeth's character.

Sustaining an appropriate line of thought

At the top of the critical essay paper are printed five bullet points on which your essay will be assessed. The first of these refers to 'sustaining an appropriate line of thought'. This means that you must present a logical argument.

Logical thinking means drawing valid conclusions from the information available. It involves putting your points into a sequence that makes sense so that if A is true and B is true then it follows that C is true.

For example:

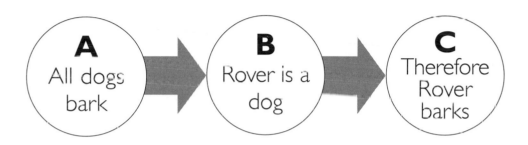

Is this logical?

In the same way, when writing a critical essay, each statement should lead on from the previous one.

Each paragraph should build on the previous one and take the argument a stage further until the conclusion is reached.

Stepping stones or staircases?

The connection between ideas should not be like stepping stones – going from one to the next to the next in a straight line:

Rather, your ideas should be linked like a staircase, taking the reader step by step towards a destination – the conclusion of the argument:

> **Tip!**
>
> Don't *list* points – *link* them.

For Practice 16

The following seven sentences could be combined into a single paragraph dealing with the theme of Macbeth's ambition to be king.

However, they do not make sense because they are not presented in a logical order.

- Rewrite them in a proper sequence so that one point leads on to the next.

- Begin by deciding which sentence could act as the topic sentence that begins the paragraph.

1   At first Macbeth feels that if this is his destiny, it will come about naturally.

2   Macbeth's ambition to be king of Scotland becomes increasingly strong in the course of the first act of the play.

3   It is clear, then, that even before Lady Macbeth puts pressure on him in Act 1 Scene 7, the ambitious side of his nature has already taken him closer to the decision to murder the king.

4   'If chance will have me king, why, chance may crown me / Without my stir.'

5   However, when King Duncan announces that his son Malcolm is to be the next king, Macbeth finds it increasingly difficult to hide his 'black and deep desires'.

6   Early on, the witches predict that Macbeth will become king.

7   For example, when Lady Macbeth hints that Duncan's arrival at Macbeth's castle might provide an ideal opportunity to kill him, Macbeth, instead of rejecting the suggestion outright, says 'we will speak further'.

For Practice 17

Read and discuss the following extracts from essays written by Higher English students.

Give each one a mark out of ten according to how well-structured the paragraph is.

Points to consider:

- Does each point arise logically out of the previous one?
- Are statements backed up with evidence?
- Are valid conclusions drawn from the evidence?
- Are points *linked* rather than *listed*?
- Does the paragraph develop in the way the topic sentence leads you to expect?

I Macbeth's soliloquy at the start of Act 1 Scene 7 clearly reveals the dilemma he is facing. On the one hand, his conscience suggests to him many reasons why he should not kill King Duncan. For example, he is Duncan's 'kinsman and subject', and as such he should be loyal to the king. Moreover, because Duncan is visiting Macbeth's castle, Macbeth is his host and should therefore:

> 'against the murderer shut the door
>
> Not bear the knife myself.'

On the other hand, Macbeth cannot control his desire to seize the throne for himself:

> 'I have no spur to prick the sides of my intent, but only
>
> Vaulting ambition.'

Thus, while reason tells Macbeth that murdering the king is wrong, emotion pulls him in the opposite direction.

Mark out of ten	Strengths	Weaknesses

2 In 'Snake', D.H. Lawrence describes how he admired a snake that came to drink at his water trough in Sicily when it was very hot and dry:

> 'Must I confess how I liked him,
> How glad I was he had come like a guest in quiet, to drink at
> My water trough.'

D.H. Lawrence uses a simile to describe the snake as:

> 'Like a king in exile.'

D.H. Lawrence throws a log to frighten the snake away:

> 'I picked up a clumsy log
> And threw it at the water-trough
> with a clatter.'

The effect of this is that the snake darts off 'like lightning' into a crack in the wall. Here the poet has also used a good simile.

When the snake arrived at the water trough the poet described its movements in detail using alliteration:

> 'He sipped with his straight mouth,
> Softly drank through his straight gums, into his long slack body,
> Silently.'

The repeated 's' sound here resembles the shape of the snake.

After throwing the log at the snake, D.H. Lawrence immediately regrets it:

> 'And immediately I regretted it.'

➔

Mark out of ten	Strengths	Weaknesses

3 In *Lord of the Flies* by William Golding, Ralph and Jack come into conflict. The book is about a group of boys who end up on a deserted island after a plane crash. One of the other boys is a fat boy called Piggy. Ralph is unkind to him at first because he reveals his nickname Piggy to the others after Piggy asked him not to. This made me dislike Ralph. Piggy is envious of Ralph because Ralph is a good swimmer, but he is not allowed to swim because he has asthma. Jack is also horrible to Piggy, which causes conflict. He calls him 'Fatty' and steals his glasses. One of Jack's friends, Roger, kills Piggy in the end, although Ralph has become friends with Piggy by then and tries to help him.

Mark out of ten	Strengths	Weaknesses

4 Fate is an important theme in *Romeo and Juliet* by the renowned dramatist William Shakespeare. The story begins with the prologue, which tells us that fate will be an important theme: 'from forth the fatal loins of these two foes'. Romeo and Juliet come from two equal families in Verona, Italy: 'two families both alike in dignity'. However, the families are forever at war with one another: 'two foes'. The families would never agree to a marriage between the two lovers, so it is obviously fate that makes them fall in love. The prologue contains a lot of words to do with fate: 'fatal, misadventured, star-crossed and death-marked'. Thus, the audience know to expect fate to be an important theme in the play proper.

Mark out of ten	Strengths	Weaknesses

5 The title of Liz Lochhead's 'Revelation' is appropriate to the theme and the text as a whole. The poem describes an episode in a young girl's life. While calling at a farm to collect eggs and milk, she was taken to see the farm's black bull, which was kept chained in an outhouse. The powerful and threatening nature of the bull is a 'revelation' to her of the darker side of life in general, leading to a loss of her childhood innocence.

The first 'revelation' is her sighting of the animal, which she calls a 'monster', a word that sums up not only its huge size but its intimidating and almost other-worldly presence. The first verse is also a 'revelation' of the horrified fascination the girl feels for the creature as she discloses how all her senses are alerted. Because it is very dark in the outhouse and the bull himself is black, touch and smell are the first senses to come into play, shown by the phrase 'hot reek'. These short, spiky-sounding words help us imagine how the overpowering smell suddenly strikes her. While visually the bull is still a vague outline, described as a 'big bulk' with edges 'merging with the darkness', the sounds come loud and clear in a phrase made dramatic with alliteration and onomatopoeia: 'he roared his rage'. Onomatopoeia is again used in the words 'trampling and clanking', conveying an immense energy that is also expressed in 'tossed' and 'jerk'. Although she describes him childishly as something 'to be really scared of', we also sense her excitement as her senses are stirred and an awareness of a new aspect of life dawns on her. Thus the 'revelation' of the bull is also a revelation of the girl's response.

Mark out of ten	Strengths	Weaknesses

Writing the concluding paragraph

> What we call the beginning is often the end. And to make an end
> is to make a beginning. The end is where we start from.
>
> *(T.S. Eliot, 1888–1965)*

The concluding paragraph of a critical essay is as important as the introductory one.

- The introduction should outline what the essay *is going to discuss*.
- The conclusion should outline what the essay *has discussed*.

The concluding paragraph *should not*

✗ bring in something new that hasn't been mentioned before

✗ end with a detailed point or an example.

The concluding paragraph *should*

✔ refer back to the words of the question

✔ follow on logically from what has been said earlier

✔ sum up the main points of the essay.

The conclusion is the final impression you leave with the marker – your last chance to persuade them that you deserve a good mark!

Pages 50–52 explained how to write an introduction to an answer on 'a poem with a specific setting', based on Norman MacCaig's 'Brooklyn Cop'. (Look back to remind yourself of the question and read the sample introduction again.)

Here's how the essay might end:

Linking word 'thus' indicates a conclusion

Reference back to the question ('setting')

Thus, through using imagery and word choice to give a detailed description of the setting in which the Brooklyn cop operates, MacCaig also succeeds in conveying a powerful message about the harm that violence can do to a society.

'Imagery' and 'word choice' — two of the main techniques discussed in detail in the course of the essay

Sums up the main point that has been argued in the essay

For Practice 18

Discuss how successful each of the following examples would be as the final paragraph in a critical essay.

1 In the last verse of 'Snake', the poet expresses his regret at having driven the snake away from his water trough. He feels he has missed an opportunity and has something to make up for. The word 'expiate' means to apologise for and to make amends for something you have done that you wish you hadn't.

2 In the course of the novel *The Prime of Miss Jean Brodie*, the relationship between Sandy and Miss Brodie changes from one of loyalty to one of dishonesty and betrayal. The author conveys this development through the use of features of style such as conversational tone, irony, repetition and word choice.

3 In conclusion, this essay has shown how the content or atmosphere of the scene or section of the play provides an effective starting point for the development of the characters and theme.

→

4   *Never Let Me Go* by Kazuo Ishiguro is an incredibly emotional novel that with its examination of human cloning brilliantly questions morals within medical science and the apathy and passiveness that, as in the case of the Holocaust and Rwanda, leads to the death of millions of people because no one would stand up for their rights. Through language and characterisation, the reader is drawn into the lives of the characters and feels the injustice along with them.

(This novel is about cloning human beings for the purpose of providing body parts for future surgery. The essay looked at the author's treatment of this moral issue.)

I   Do you think the candidate's word choice is completely appropriate?

2   How clearly has she presented her final evaluation of the novel?

5   Malcolm's final summing up of Macbeth as a 'butcher' is accurate in view of his many murders, but in the scenes leading up to Macbeth's death, the audience can see traces of his former conscience in his reluctance to kill Macduff, admitting: 'my soul is too much charged with blood of thine already'. Macbeth's bravado in his last moments: 'I will not yield / to kiss the ground before young Malcolm's feet' is stirring in its pride, and we can sympathise with his awareness that he will never have the usual joys of old age: 'Honour, love, obedience, troops of friends'. Ultimately, the audience is aware of Macbeth as a great man who has been driven by his ambition to choose evil over good, and has thus forfeited all that is really important in life

(This essay looked at the development of the character of Macbeth in the play, from hero to villain.)

I   How well does this conclusion sum up the argument of the essay?

2   Does the candidate make his own view clear?

Part Three

Improving Your Style and Expression

Punctuation

Spelling

Style and Expression

By now, you should have a good idea of how to go about

- preparing your literature texts

- writing in a way that is relevant to the question

- showing your knowledge of the text

- backing up your comments with evidence

- giving your essay a structure.

However, a look at a past Higher exam paper will show one other 'performance criterion' that is taken into account by the markers:

…the quality of your written expression and the technical accuracy of your writing…

Does that mean that even if I write about my text in detail and answer the question, I could still fail if I make punctuation or spelling mistakes?

In a word: yes!

Obviously, some minor errors are to be expected when an essay is written under a time limit in an exam. However, if the punctuation, spelling and style of expression are consistently poor throughout the whole essay, it could fail.

This section of the book is designed to help you improve these aspects of your work without going into all the technicalities of grammar.

Punctuation

Why bother about punctuation?

To put it at its simplest, punctuation means dividing words into groups. The way the words are separated into sentences can have just as big an effect on the meaning of the statement as the words themselves.

Punctuation is one of the basic skills of English writing. The content of an essay might be quite acceptable, but if the sentences are all run together without full stops it is unlikely to reach pass standard.

Full stops at the end of sentences

Full stops are the most important of all punctuation marks. When you come to the end of a completed statement – a group of words that makes sense standing on its own – then you should put a full stop.

This is something that you've been told since primary school, nevertheless, people still find it difficult, this is because they tend to allow their thoughts to run ahead, this means that one sentence often merges into the next, the writer forgets to put in full stops.

Did you notice that there was something wrong with that paragraph?

Try reading it out loud and you will find that you naturally pause at the end of each completed statement. This is where the full stops should go.

The paragraph above should read as follows:

> This is something that you've been told since primary school. Nevertheless, people still find it difficult. This is because they tend to allow their thoughts to run ahead. This means that one sentence often merges into the next. The writer forgets to put in full stops.

For Practice 1

This paragraph describes a game of rugby. Rewrite it, putting in full stops at the end of completed statements.

> The second half began with three points to Scotland, secured from a penalty kick, the Scottish forwards seemed to have been given a new lease of life, they carried the game well into enemy territory, the gold jerseys of the Kangaroos were now soiled, the dark blue of the Scots made them look the less bedraggled side, all but Galt, his duty had been that of desperate defence and he had suffered for it, his jersey was half torn off his back and his shorts were in ribbons, he limped heavily and his face looked as if it had been ground into the mud of his native land, this made him feel dull and stupid as if he had been slightly concussed.

Conjunctions

Even though an essay might have the full stops in the right place, the sentences may still not 'flow' very well. Too many short sentences, or too many sentences of a similar length, will give a piece of writing a monotonous effect.

For this reason, you should vary your sentence lengths by using joining words (conjunctions) to join some short sentences into longer ones.

Here are four points to remember about conjunctions.

1 The simplest conjunctions are 'and' and 'but'. These are obviously very useful words, but you should not overuse them.

2 Other useful joining words are:

although		when
	until	while
because		if
	unless	as
before		after

3 A conjunction can either be placed *between* two sentences

> We will be leaving for the airport *when* we have finished packing our cases.

or at the beginning

> *When* we have finished packing our cases, we will be leaving for the airport.

4 'So' is a particularly overused conjunction. This is all right in informal writing, but it should be avoided in a formal essay. Instead of saying 'so' in the middle of two sentences, put 'as' at the start of the first one.

For example, in a piece of formal writing it is better to write

> As the writer is trying to describe the sound of the wind, he uses figures of speech such as onomatopoeia and alliteration.

than

> The writer is trying to describe the sound of the wind *so* he uses figures of speech such as onomatopoeia and alliteration.

This or which?

One of the places where students wrongly put a comma instead of a full stop is when a sentence begins with the word 'this'. In an essay on poetry, one candidate wrote:

> In the first verse the poet uses a simile, this gives the reader a closer picture of what the animal looked like.

There are two possibilities here:

1 Put a full stop after 'simile' and a capital letter at 'this':

> In the first verse the poet uses a simile. This gives the reader a closer picture of what the animal looked like.

2 Replace the word 'this' with the relative pronoun 'which':

> In the first verse the poet uses a simile, which gives the reader a closer picture of what the animal looked like.

Colons and semi-colons

Students often confuse these two. A colon is the one made up of two dots (:) and a semi-colon combines a dot and a comma (;).

They have different functions.

A colon introduces a list or an explanation:

> There can only be one explanation of his behaviour: he is completely mad.

A semi-colon marks the end of a sentence, but less firmly than a full stop does. It is most often used where one sentence is closely related to the one that follows it. For example, the second one might provide a contrast or balance to the previous one:

> My parents like to get up early at the weekend; I would rather have a long lie.

Remember: when a semi-colon is used, it would often be quite acceptable to put a full stop instead, but it would be wrong to put a comma.

Spelling

This is obviously a big topic and there is not space to cover it thoroughly here. However, there are four categories of words that you should concentrate on.

1. Favourite errors

Every student has particular words that he or she always finds hard to spell. Make a list of these, underline the difficult part (for example double letters or 'i before e') and copy them out until you remember them.

Most people would include words like the following on their lists:

receive
development
necessary
occasionally
recommend
sufficient
tomorrow
beginning
independent
immediately
separate
achievement
belief
thought
business
usually
knowledge

2. Words you know you will have to use

In preparing for a critical essay, there are certain technical terms that are bound to come up. You will have used them in practice essays and are likely to use them in your exam answers. Again, write them out until you remember them. For example:

character
argument
soliloquy
simile
sentence
humour/humorous
statement

Go through your notes on each text and make a list of any words that present difficulty. For example, if you are studying *Macbeth*, you are likely at some point to refer to the witches' prophecies. Make sure you understand the difference between the following:

prophecy
prophesy
prophecies
prophesied

The word is spelt with an 's' when it is a verb and a 'c' when it is a noun.

The witches prophesied that Macbeth would become king.

The witches made various prophecies about Macbeth's future.

3. Words you need to double-check

Many spelling errors result from carelessness rather than lack of knowledge.

Particular ones to watch out for are:

there/their/they're
wear/were/where
to/too/two
hear/here
right/write
quite/quiet
affect/effect

4. Apostrophes

Apostrophes are used to indicate:

- That a letter is missed out:

    Do not becomes **don't**.

- Ownership:

    The phone belonging to the boy becomes **the boy's phone**.

    If the word is plural, the apostrophe comes after the 's'.

    The boys' phones would mean that there is more than one boy and more than one phone.

- 'It's' only has an apostrophe when short for 'it is':

    It's time to go home.

Style and Expression

The best way to improve your style is to read widely and observe how skilled writers express themselves. Here are a few guidelines to follow when writing a critical essay.

1 Language should be accurate in terms of *sentence structure*, punctuation and spelling.

2 Use a *formal style*: avoid 'chatty' language, abbreviations and slang expressions.

3 Avoid using abbreviations: write 'for example' instead of 'e.g.'. Write out words like 'don't', 'can't' and 'isn't' in full – 'do not', 'cannot', 'is not'.

4 Instead of saying 'you', refer to 'the reader' if you are talking about a novel or poem, or 'the audience' if you are writing about a play.

5 Avoid overused expressions like '*a lot*' (say 'much'/'many'/'a number of'/'several') and '*thing*' (be precise: instead of saying 'one thing about the poem that appealed to me was…', say 'one feature/aspect…').

6 Avoid text speak – 'U', etc.

7 Avoid emotive language ('over-the-top' expressions of feeling). Don't say things like 'this was a brilliant book' or 'I found this poem fantastic'. There is no need to commend established writers: 'the amazing playwright, William Shakespeare'; 'the very talented poet John Keats', etc.

8 Do not be negative (for example, 'this book was boring'). Texts will have been chosen for their literary merit and you should show awareness of this. Negative comments betray lack of appreciation and understanding.

9 The occasional use of the first person 'I' is fine, because it shows genuine *personal* response (for example, 'at this point in the novel I felt sympathetic towards Piggy because of the way the others boys treated him'). However, you should not overdo this. Instead, use words that express your response such as 'moving', 'poignant', 'disturbing'.

10 Aim for variety of style: refer to the words of the question, but do not simply repeat the exact words too often. Use synonyms.

11 The first time you refer to the author, use his/her full name. Thereafter use the surname only, and never the first name alone. Alternatively, say 'the writer', 'the poet', etc.

12 Make use of the linking expressions explained on page 78. These help the argument of the essay to flow.

13 Sentences should be neither too long nor too short. Long-winded sentences lead to confusion. In general, try to make one point in one sentence then start a new one.

14 Avoid expressions like 'as I said earlier' (this suggests that the essay is poorly structured and is repeating itself) or 'the author uses a good quote to show that...' (Authors do not write 'quotes'; *you* are the one who is quoting.)

For Practice 2

Here are some extracts from essays written by exam candidates. Identify the weaknesses in the style of writing by referring to the numbers above. For example, if you feel the extract is too informal and uses emotive language, write down numbers 2 and 7 in the box provided.

Next, choose one of the examples and rewrite it, improving the style by

- correcting the punctuation
- correcting the spelling
- joining sentences with conjunctions or with 'which'
- making informal expressions more formal
- avoiding repetition
- improving the expression in any other ways as required.

1 Shakespeare introduces the character of Macbeth very highly, he describes him as 'brave Macbeth' this emphasises his loyalty that he has given a lot of loyalty to his country and king. And so as we have been introduced to Macbeth in such a high standard any mistakes or wrong decisions that he makes would have to be caused by a major flaw in his personality.

2 When Romeo meets Juliet at the ball he falls in love with her and she with him. He instantly forgets about Rosaline who he used to fancy. He's quite shocked when Friar Lawrence hints that he has been up to something with Rosaline: 'I have forgot that name and that name's woe', and makes it clear he doesn't want to talk about her.

3 A poem that would particularly appeal to a teenage reader is 'Tich Miller' by Wendy Cope. Because the poem is short it doesn't have time to get boring, which makes it particularly appeal to a teenage reader. Because the language is simple it is easier to understand than most poems Tich Miller 'had one foot three sizes larger than the other'. This comment is easy to understand, which would particularly appeal to a teenager reader. It also gives you a laugh, which is also something which appeals to a teenage reader.

→

4 Macbeth, who is travelling back to his castle, after the battle against the Norwegians and the Scottish traitors where he killed Macdonwald and helped the Scots to victory, along with Banquo, who is with him, they then meet the witches who Macbeth very much wants to believe in their promises while Banquo is more cautious:

> The instruments of darkness tell us truths…to betray us in deepest consequence.

5 At the beginning of the play, Romeo is in love with Rosaline. Rosaline has vowed never to marry. She will never love Romeo in return. Romeo finds love confusing. He speaks in paradoxes, which shows this: 'feather of lead, bright smoke, cold fire'. Benvolio suggests he will forget Rosaline if he examines other beauties: 'examine other beauties'. Romeo does not agree. He goes to the ball hoping to see Rosaline. Then fate steps in and he falls in love with Juliet.

6 There are 4 reasons why Macbeth decides he shouldn't kill Duncan, (a) he is his kinsman, (b) he is his subject, (c) he is his host, (d) Duncan has many virtues. The only reason he should kill him is (e) he has a powerful ambition, 'vaulting ambition'.

7 'Tich Miller' by Wendy Cope is a superb poem by the excellent British poet Wendy Cope. It is truly hilarious, which should appeal to teenage readers. The line, 'Tich Miller had one foot three sizes bigger than the other' had me and all my class in stitches. We could imagine this funny looking young girl with broken glasses and one big foot and one little one. But it is devastating at the end when she says, 'Tich died when she was twelve'. There were definitely a few tears for her. Wendy has written the poem in a really great way all through.

Part Four

Sample Essays

Model Essay on 'Brooklyn Cop'

Your Turn To Be a Marker

Some of the exercises in this book have asked you to criticise extracts from other students' work that illustrate good and bad practice.

In this final section you will find:

- A 'model essay' on 'Brooklyn Cop', which should give you an idea of the standard to aim for.

- A checklist of features of a good Higher English critical essay.

- Some sample essays, which allow *you* to try being a marker.

Model Essay on 'Brooklyn Cop'

The essay that follows puts into practice all the skills you have studied in the course of this book. The notes in the margins indicate what each section of the essay is attempting to do.

The essay is an answer to the following question:

> Choose a poem in which a specific setting is strongly evoked.
>
> Show how the poet creates this sense of place and/or time, and then discuss the relative importance of the setting to the poem as a whole.

Remember, too, that the Higher paper includes the following instruction:

> Answers to questions on poetry should address relevantly the central concern(s)/theme(s) of the text(s) and be supported by reference to appropriate poetic techniques such as: imagery, verse form, structure, mood, tone, sound, rhythm, rhyme, characterisation, contrast, setting, symbolism, word choice…

Warning!

Using model essays wrongly can be very bad for your exam results. You should never try to 'learn' a model essay (from this book or from any other source, such as the Internet) for an English exam, because you would be copying someone else's work (*plagiarism*) and you would fail your whole exam because of it. Model essays are useful to help you appreciate how such essays are marked and why, but your examination essays *must be your own work*.

Name of text and author

Brief summary of poem

Reference to words from the question that set the task (namely setting and its importance to the poem)

A poem that strongly evokes a specific setting is 'Brooklyn Cop' by Norman MacCaig. The poet describes the dangers faced by a New York policeman on a day-to-day basis and shows that he has had to develop a toughness and brutality in order to survive in this place. A strong impression of the violent atmosphere in the Brooklyn area is conveyed, which is of paramount importance in portraying the policeman. By establishing the setting through the use of vivid imagery and word choice, MacCaig makes it clear that the policeman's personality and physical appearance have been shaped by the violence surrounding him.

Reference to words of the question

The last sentence makes it clear that key aspects such as 'setting' and 'imagery' mentioned in the question will be examined in more detail in the rest of the essay

Topic sentence picks up the idea of a violent society mentioned in the introduction

MacCaig's word choice and use of imagery create a picture of a violent society. The poet describes how the police officer

> 'walks the sidewalk and the
>   thin tissue over violence.'

Quotation provides an example

This sentence develops the previous point

A 'thin tissue' is obviously a very fragile and easily removed covering; in the same way, the veneer of civilisation is completely powerless to suppress the violence that erupts in the streets on a daily basis. The speed at which this can happen is emphasised in the second verse, which considers what could happen

> 'should the tissue tear, should he
>   plunge through into violence.'

Comment on the quotation.

Further quotation

→

The word 'plunge' implies a sudden and brutal immersion in the violent atmosphere. The references to the names of individual locations ('Phoebe's Whamburger' and 'Louie's Place') emphasise how well the policeman knows his beat and how familiar he is with the trouble spots. The neologism 'Whamburger' combines a colloquial term for a vicious blow with the word 'hamburger' and suggests that this café is notorious for fighting. This may even suggest that, like food, violence is a daily necessity to some of the inhabitants of this area.

Detailed comment on word choice

Argument is strengthened by a further example of word choice, again followed by detailed comment

For Discussion

- Look back over the previous paragraph (beginning 'MacCaig's word choice …'). What are the three key words or expressions in the opening sentence?

- Trace how these are developed in detail in the rest of the paragraph.

Bridging sentence: 'this violent setting' points back to the previous paragraph while the second half of the sentence points forward to the next topic

The poet's description of this violent setting is important to the poem as a whole because the policeman is entirely shaped by his surroundings. His appearance reflects his toughness, emphasised by the opening simile 'built like a gorilla but less timid'. As a gorilla is not a timid creature, the hyperbole used here emphasises how tough and imposing the policeman is. The fact that the word 'gorilla' is used three times in the poem makes this comparison our dominant impression of the cop. Similarly,

Quotation and comment. Reference to 'simile' and 'hyperbole' shows knowledge of appropriate technical terms.

Linking word indicating that a similar idea is being added on

→

'steak-coloured' has connotations of something raw, tough and animal-like. Daily encounters with violence have left their mark on him in the form of scars: 'two hieroglyphs in his face'. Hieroglyphs are a primitive way of communicating in writing; in the same way, the scars suggest a message is written on the face of the policeman for all to see - that he will take on the violent men at their own game.

Quotation and comment

Further comment on imagery

Although some of the exaggeration in the imagery seems humorous, MacCaig can also be serious, fully recognising that going to work each morning involves great danger for the policeman, with a considerable risk that he will not return in the evening:

'This morning
 when he said, "See you, babe" to his
 wife, he hoped it, he truly hoped it.'

Quotation backing up statement

The repetition of 'he hoped it' stresses the genuine fear that underlines the apparently light-hearted and casual tone of his remark 'see you, babe'.

Linking word indicates that a different point is to follow

However, the poet does not only show sympathy for the policeman. The rhetorical question

Further reference to literary technique, backed up with a quotation

'And who would be who have to be
 his victims?'

→

108

Consideration of the poem 'as a whole', as expected by the question

implies that he, too, metes out violence as well as suffering it. While the poem is mainly descriptive, this line implies that MacCaig also has a message for the reader: that violence in society affects both those who break the law and those who enforce it. The tense of the verb 'have to be' and the term 'victim' suggest that all these people are caught up in a web of violence from which they cannot escape.

'Thus' indicates essay is drawing to a conclusion

Concluding paragraph summarises main points of the essay

Thus, through using imagery and word choice to give a detailed description of the setting in which the Brooklyn Cop operates, MacCaig also succeeds in conveying a powerful message about the harm that violence can do to a society.

Repetition of key words from the question

Checklist of features of a good Higher English critical essay

	Tick

The opening paragraph

- Is the text and author clearly stated in the opening sentence?
- Is the title correctly written, using capital letters and inverted commas?
- Does the introduction use words from the question?
- Does it include a brief summary of what the text is about?
- Are the key topics of the task mentioned?
- Is some indication given as to how the essay will develop?

The main body of the essay

Relevance

- The essay may begin by referring to the question, but is this relevance sustained all the way through?
- Are the words of the question referred to several times in the course of the essay, usually at the start of a paragraph?
- Does the essay discuss themes, characters, style, etc. rather than simply recounting the plot?
- If the essay is about character development, does it analyse the factors that bring about changes in the character?

Structure

- Does each paragraph begin with a clear topic sentence?
- Does the topic sentence relate to the question?
- Does it point forwards to what is to be examined next?
- Does the essay have a logical progression? In other words, does one point lead to the next, which leads to the next and so on?
- Does the candidate use linking sentences to bridge from one paragraph to the next?
- Is there a clear conclusion or summing up that refers to the question?

→

Checklist of features of a good Higher English critical essay

Tick

Use of evidence

- Does the essay have a wide range of reference to most of the text, rather than focusing only on (for example) the opening chapters or scenes?

- Are quotations used?

- Are they worded accurately?

- When a statement is made, is it backed up with evidence?

- Are the quotations placed in context? Is it clear which character is speaking and where the words come in the context of the whole text?

- Are quotations followed by at least one meaningful comment?

- Is there variety in the types of evidence provided? For example, references to incidents or events can support a point as well as direct quotations.

Style and expression

- Is punctuation used correctly? In particular, do sentences end with full stops rather than running into each other ('comma splice')?

- Are sentences of an appropriate length to make the point clear?

- Is spelling correct?

- Is the essay written in an appropriately formal style?

- Is the language free of abbreviations and slang expressions?

- Does the essay refer to the words of the question without repeating them too often in exactly the same way?

- Are linking words and phrases used to give continuity?

Don't forget!

The checklist of features summarises all the essay-writing skills you have studied in this book.

Next time you have to write a critical essay, use this checklist to assess your own work.

If you can say 'yes' to all the points on the checklist, your essay should score a good mark!

Your Turn To Be a Marker

Assessing other pupils' critical essays can help you to become alert to common faults which you will then be much less likely to commit yourself!

Look out for these common errors of approach:

✗ Reproducing an essay that has been prepared earlier, on a question which may be similar to, but not exactly the same as, the question being attempted. Frequently, candidates give themselves away by including phrases from questions asked in earlier years instead of focusing on the key words of the question that they are meant to be answering!

✗ Including material that may be intelligent, perceptive and accurate, which shows understanding of the text, but has nothing to do with the question.

✗ Retelling too much of the plot of a play, novel or short story.

✗ Providing a general, verse-by-verse, commentary on a poem.

✗ Failing to answer the whole question, which will often ask candidates to fulfil more than one task. Questions that firstly ask candidates to look at a scene of a play, or an episode in a novel, or the opening of a text, will almost always go on to ask how this impacts on their 'understanding of the text as a whole'. Merely writing one or two sentences summarising the remainder of the plot will not fulfil this requirement.

For Practice 1: Sample Essays on 'Snake'

In 2007, this was one of the poetry questions:

> **Choose a poem in which there is effective use of one or more of the following: verse form, rhythm, rhyme, repetition, sound.**
>
> **Show how the poet effectively uses the feature(s) to enhance your appreciation of the poem as a whole.**

Certain candidates wrote on the poem 'Snake' by D.H. Lawrence. Here are the first four stanzas of the poem which are analysed in the extracts that follow.

Snake

A snake came to my water-trough
On a hot, hot day, and I in pyjamas for the heat,
To drink there.

In the deep, strange-scented shade of the great dark
carob-tree
I came down the steps with my pitcher
And must wait, must stand and wait, for there he was
at the trough before me.

He reached down from a fissure in the earth wall in
the gloom
And trailed his yellow-brown slackness soft-bellied down,
over the edge of the stone trough
And rested his throat upon the stone bottom,
And where the water had dripped from the tap,
in a small clearness,
He sipped with his straight mouth,
Softly drank through his straight gums, into his slack
long body,
Silently.

Someone was before me at my water-trough,
And I, like a second-comer, waiting.

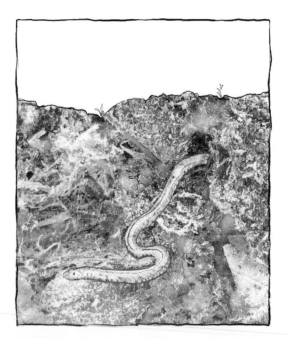

Reading the question

The question contains what is called a '*closed list*'. This means that the candidates *had* to deal with one or more of those five features specified in the question. However, while the focus had to be on one or more of these five features, the answer had to show how they 'enhanced your appreciation as a whole'. Therefore, the features had to be related to the ideas of the poem.

What you have to do

This poem was an excellent choice for the question. But how good were the essays? The following three responses all deal with these opening stanzas only. Once you have read them, assess them according to the checklist on pages 110–111. You could do this exercise either individually or in groups.

Answer A

A poem in which there is a noticeable change of mood at one or more points in the poem is 'Snake' by D.H. Lawrence. The verse form, rhythm, repetition and sound in the poem enhanced my appreciation of the poem. The poem is about a man who comes on a poisonous snake in his garden. At first the poet is shocked, but then intrigued. He watches the snake with interest. However, as he watches, he recollects that the snake is dangerous and throws a stick at it. He then has another change of mood as he feels ashamed of trying to harm it.

The poet begins the poem with a matter of fact tone, saying the snake came to the water-trough 'to drink' as it was a 'hot, hot day'. This seems an obvious thing to do, and we feel he does not grudge the snake the water as he feels very hot himself: 'in pyjamas for the heat'. The descriptive expression 'deep strange-scented shade of the great dark carob-tree' creates a tranquil, peaceful mood and so we are not surprised when the poet responds in a peaceful way. He treats the snake with respect as if it is human, and feels he must 'stand and wait'. Calling the snake 'he' emphasises this respect.

However, there is also some tension in this part of the poem. Certain words reveal disgust at details of the appearance of the snake, such as 'slackness', 'soft-bellied' and 'straight mouth'. We get the idea of the man holding himself in check, especially in the line, 'And I, like a second-comer, waiting'. The pauses from the commas in this line, which comes before a break, give the impression of something about to happen, and prepare us for a change of mood.

Answer B

A poem in which there is effective use of verse form, rhythm, repetition and sound that enhance my appreciation is 'Snake' by D.H. Lawrence. D.H. Lawrence was writing in the early years of the twentieth century. His personal life was rather turbulent. He fell in love with a married woman, Frieda, who left her husband and children to go and live with him. When her husband divorced her, D.H. Lawrence and Frieda felt forced to go abroad to live as divorce was not acceptable in British society at that time. D.H. Lawrence felt sympathy with outcasts and underdogs because of this, and his attitude to the snake in the poem could be seen as an example of this. The poem is set in Sicily in Italy, which is one of the countries in which D.H. Lawrence and his wife lived in voluntary exile for some years.

The poem is set in a typical Italian garden, and Lawrence provides detail that builds up the atmosphere effectively: we can clearly imagine the picturesque flight of steps, the lovely scent of the shady 'great dark carob-tree' and the stone trough with its dripping tap. The snake is beautifully described, and although most readers may hate snakes, a peaceful impression is created as the snake moves gently and is so relaxed and quiet: he 'trailed' his body slowly, and 'rested' his head and takes the water in little mouthfuls: 'sipped', showing he is in no hurry and not at all afraid of the poet who is standing watching him. I found it quite humorous that the poet even feels he has to wait in line for his own tap, as he is the 'second-comer'.

Answer C

A poem in which there is effective use of verse form, rhythm, repetition and sound that enhance my appreciation is 'Snake' by D.H. Lawrence. This poem, describing the poet's encounter with a snake, contrasts man's natural responses with his learned responses. The fact that the natural responses are the ones that the poet shows should be trusted is mirrored by the poet's choice of free verse, which gives the poem an appropriate spontaneity that would not have been the case with a more rigid, rhymed verse form.

Repetition is a technique used in many places to give an intensity to the expression. The setting is immediately evoked with the phrase 'on a hot, hot day' and the word 'heat' at the end of the line focuses again on this detail of the weather, which builds up an atmosphere of tension as the man sights the poisonous snake, although an anticlimax is achieved in the short third line when he notes it has only come to the water-trough 'to drink there'. The use of long lines and enjambment in the following section creates a slow steady rhythm as if mimicking the poet coming down the steps, while the punctuation is used effectively together with repetition to emphasise how the man stops short in shock, as most people would at the sight of a snake: 'must wait, must stand and wait'. The incremental repetition of the second phrase, with the addition of '…stand and…', has a slightly humorous effect as if the man feels aggrieved at having to take his turn at his own water tap.

The use of extra-long lines and enjambment is again deployed in the verse describing the snake slithering down, and this effectively suggests its elongated body: 'trailed his yellow-brown slackness soft-bellied down…' Sound is used most effectively in this section: the sibilance created by the alliteration of 's' in words like 'sipped…straight…softly…silently' is appropriate in evoking the slightly disturbing presence of a snake.

Tick one or more boxes in the checklist as you think appropriate, and then provide comments to justify your choice underneath.

Checklist

1 Is there any evidence that this is a pre-prepared answer based on a different question? (Check poetry sections in your past papers.)

Answer A	Answer B	Answer C

Comments:

_____

_____

_____

_____

_____

2 Does the answer include material that is intelligent, perceptive and accurate, which shows understanding of the text, but has nothing to do with the question?

Answer A	Answer B	Answer C

Comments:

_____

_____

_____

_____

_____

→

Checklist *continued*

3 Does the answer provide a general, verse-by-verse, commentary on the poem without focusing on what is asked in the question?

Answer A	Answer B	Answer C

Comments:

_____

_____

_____

_____

_____

_____

_____

4 Does the answer give a relevant, well-structured response to the task?

Answer A	Answer B	Answer C

Comments:

_____

_____

_____

_____

_____

_____

_____

Turn to page 126 for a commentary on these essays. Compare it with your own comments.

For Practice 2: Sample Essays on Romeo and Juliet

This exercise would be best done in a group, so that you can argue the merits of each essay. It is possible to mark an essay even if you do not know the text.

Each of the essays is attempting to answer the following question:

> Choose a play in which there is a scene that provides a clear turning point in the drama.
>
> Explain why it is a turning point and go on to discuss the importance of the scene to your appreciation of the play as a whole.

Note the three strands of the task in this question that candidates must include in their essays:

- Identify a scene that is a genuine turning point in a play. Briefly justify the choice of scene.

- Explain why it is a turning point – this will involve a contrast of before and after the scene to show evidence of a change of direction.

- Focus on the scene itself and how it is important to the appreciation of the whole play – this will involve reference to the 'main concerns' of the play.

They will also have to end with

- a general conclusion.

What you have to do

Read each essay and assess it according to the 'Checklist of features of a good Higher English critical essay' on pages 110–111.

Discuss your findings in a group and agree on an assessment of each essay. You might use the grids on page 125 to record your comments. Then compare your assessments with those of other groups. You could finally look at the short commentary on the essays, which is on page 127–128.

(All factual information on the text in each essay is correct. All quotations are accurate. There are no spelling or punctuation errors, but you may wish to comment on expression.)

Essay 1: Duncan's essay

In *Romeo and Juliet* by William Shakespeare, a clear turning point in the play comes in Act 3 Scene 1. The play concerns the fate of two young lovers, whose families, the Capulets and the Montagues, are engaged in a long-standing feud. In this scene, which follows the secret marriage of the lovers, Romeo kills Juliet's cousin, Tybalt, in revenge for Tybalt killing his friend, Mercutio. As a result, Romeo is exiled and a chain of events is set in motion that eventually leads to the deaths of both lovers. The scene sheds more light on Romeo's character and shows how fateful an error of judgement can be in the context of the feud.

Act 3 Scene 1 represents a turning point in several ways. Firstly, it marks a change in the fortunes of Romeo and Juliet. Although the audience are warned in the prologue that the feud will only be ended by the deaths of the 'star-crossed lovers', this tends to be lost sight of in the first part of the play. The audience get swept along by their romantic passion, illogically hoping for a happy ending, despite some misgivings from Juliet and the Friar about the rash speed of events, which, in Juliet's words, seems 'too like the lightning'. The marriage is swiftly arranged with the help of the Nurse, leading Juliet to exclaim, 'Hie to high fortune!' because she is confident of a happy outcome. However, these words prepare us for the turning point: the idea of fortune being 'high' has connotations of the medieval idea of Fortune's wheel, which is destined to descend after reaching its high point. When Romeo murders Juliet's cousin, we know that a happy ending is impossible.

In terms of the structure of the plot, the scene is also a turning point. Before the scene, the plot focuses on Romeo and Juliet falling in love, which culminates in their marriage, despite the great feud. After this scene, Capulet's plan to arrange a marriage between Juliet and Count Paris dominates the action. This is destined to end in tragedy, because Juliet is already married. The Nurse withdraws her support and Friar Lawrence's plan for Juliet to feign death misfires when Romeo, too, is deceived by it.

A third way in which this scene provides a turning point concerns the change of mood brought about by the violence. The mood in the first two acts is predominantly light-hearted, with the characters of Mercutio and the Nurse

→

providing much comedy in the form of amusing speeches and monologues. The death of Mercutio ends the humorous banter. Before the turning point, the Nurse is Juliet's closest ally, while after it she betrays her in advising her to marry Paris bigamously, leading Juliet to curse her: 'ancient damnation!' In addition, Benvolio, whose name suggests that he personifies good will, does not appear again after this scene, as if the spirit of good will has left the play and given way to malice. This malice is to be found in Lady Capulet's cries for vengeance, and in the Nurse's sour comment that 'there's no faith, no honesty in men', which briefly even turns Juliet against Romeo: 'O serpent heart'. The later mood may be summed up in Romeo's words, 'more dark and dark our woes'.

The scene also contributes significantly to our appreciation of the play as a whole. The feud is an important element of the play that overshadows all of the action. It is symbolised in this scene by the hot, tense July weather at the start of the scene, when Benvolio begs Mercutio to go home, in order to avoid violence: 'now these hot days is the mad blood stirring'. The use of monosyllables in Benvolio's speech helps build tension. The feud motivates both Mercutio and Tybalt, and the good will of Benvolio is powerless against it. Romeo is sucked back into the destructive vendetta when Mercutio dies.

Another way in which the scene is important is to our understanding of the development of Romeo's character. At the start of the play he is presented as impetuous and even fickle as his affections are transferred abruptly from Rosaline to Juliet. His actions are equally erratic, whether he is wandering in the woods by night or climbing the Capulet orchard walls in pursuit of Juliet. In this scene, marriage to Juliet seems to have mellowed him, as he responds to Tybalt's insult of 'thou art a villain' with calm good humour: 'Villain am I none. / Therefore farewell, I see thou knowest me not.' However, after Mercutio is murdered, the impetuous side of Romeo's temperament again emerges as he rushes to avenge his friend, declaring: 'fire-eyed fury be my conduct, now!' He blames Juliet for making him 'effeminate', and he also blames fate: 'I am Fortune's fool', instead of accepting responsibility for his action. This fatal flaw of recklessness will lead to tragedy, as it is the same trait that leads him to rush to kill himself by Juliet's side when he believes she is dead.

➡

The final section of the scene adds to our appreciation of the play as a whole in several ways. It is like a courtroom scene with the Prince acting as judge and Benvolio as a witness. Lady Capulet comes over as harsh and vengeful as she demands Romeo's death: 'Romeo slew Tybalt – Romeo must not live!' This alienates the audience, who are aware of the irony that she is demanding the death of her son-in-law. The audience feels sympathy with Romeo, who is the object of her fierce hatred. In the later scenes of her conflict with Juliet our sympathies are therefore all on one side.

To sum up, the violence that erupts in this scene brings about a clear turning point in the play. Friar Lawrence's hopes of the 'rancour' of the feud being transformed to love are dashed. The positive, light-hearted mood changes to one of dark uncertainty. The audience comprehend fully the destructive power of the feud while appreciating that Romeo's impulsive character, as much as fate, will contribute to the catastrophe. The latter part of the scene recalls the phrase 'parents' rage' from the prologue, and reminds us that the lovers die. There will be great poignancy in watching the rest of the play as we know that the lovers' efforts to find a solution will be in vain.

Essay 2: Sarah's essay

In *Romeo and Juliet* by William Shakespeare, I think the turning point comes at the beginning of Act 3. The play is about a young man and woman whose families have been involved in a feud for many years. Romeo and Juliet met at a ball in the Capulets' house. Romeo had gate-crashed, because being a Montague he had of course not been invited. The two fell in love and got married in secret. They probably hoped that eventually their families would come round and the feud would end. However in Act 3, Juliet's cousin Tybalt kills Romeo's friend, Mercutio. Romeo then kills Tybalt. The Prince sends Romeo into exile and it all goes wrong from there.

At the start of the play, Romeo was in love with another girl, Rosaline. However, he was depressed as he was getting nowhere because she had taken a vow never to marry. Then Romeo's friend, Benvolio, persuades him to go to the Capulets' ball. Romeo agrees but only because he knows Rosaline will be there. However, at the ball, Romeo sees Juliet and falls in love with her instantly: 'she doth teach the torches to burn bright', he says. He also compares her to 'a jewel in an Ethiop's ear'. These images of light give an idea of how much he admires her beauty. They meet and talk, but are shocked when they discover who it is they have fallen in love with. Romeo leaves the ball, but he then climbs the wall into the Capulets' garden, and he finds Juliet on her balcony, speaking about him: 'Romeo, Romeo, wherefore art thou Romeo?' By the end of the night they have agreed to get married. Romeo's priest, Friar Lawrence, is to perform the ceremony. Juliet's Nurse, who is quite a funny character, helps them arrange it.

Unfortunately, Juliet's cousin, Tybalt, had recognised Romeo at the Capulets' ball and wanted to have him put out. His uncle, Juliet's father, annoyed Tybalt by telling him to leave Romeo alone, saying he had heard Romeo was 'a virtuous and well-governed youth', which seemed to hint that Tybalt was not like that. Capulet then got angry when Tybalt kept arguing and humiliated him by calling him a 'saucy boy'. Tybalt had no choice but to leave, but he swore that he would get his revenge.

→

Tybalt tried to get his revenge in Act 3 Scene 1. Romeo had by now got married to Juliet. Tybalt calls him names, which he is sure will make Romeo very angry: 'thou art a villain'. But Romeo turns his back and walks off. Meanwhile, Mercutio can't stand seeing Romeo turning his back. He steps in because he thinks Romeo's behaviour is dishonourable: 'calm, dishonourable, vile submission!' Tybalt and Mercutio now start a fight, and Romeo tries to stop it. Then Tybalt manages to stab Mercutio while Romeo is holding Mercutio back. Mercutio is angry with Romeo for interfering: 'why the devil came you between us? I was hurt under your arm'. Romeo apologises: 'I thought all for the best'. But Mercutio won't forgive him and just says, 'a plague on both your houses'. This is like a curse, because a plague would kill everyone in the house. Because Romeo and Juliet both die at the end, and they are the only children in their families, this is just like a plague because everyone will soon be dead, and so Mercutio's curse will unfortunately come true. This makes the scene a turning point.

After Mercutio dies Romeo loses his temper. He runs after Tybalt and, after a fight, kills him. Then the Prince comes in. He banishes Romeo from Verona for ever. This would seem merciful to anyone else, but Romeo doesn't see it this way because it means leaving Juliet.

The scene is very important to your appreciation of the whole play. You can understand how fights suddenly flare up, and how things happen that no one intended. Romeo did not intend to get into a fight and calls himself 'Fortune's fool', which I think he was. Fate is an important theme in *Romeo and Juliet*, and they are also unlucky in what happens next.

Romeo and Juliet spend the night together, then he goes into exile. Juliet's family now decide she should marry Count Paris. (This was mentioned at the start of the play, but Capulet said he didn't want it to happen for 2 years.) Juliet doesn't want to do this because she is already married to Romeo, although her family don't know it. The Nurse is no help and just tells her to go ahead and marry Paris, saying he will be a better husband than Romeo. However, Friar Lawrence comes up with a plan. Juliet will take a drug that will make her appear dead. She will be put in the tomb and the Friar will send a message to Romeo explaining he should come and collect her. However, it all goes wrong when Romeo hears she is dead but he doesn't get the message from the Friar. Romeo rushes back and poisons himself, then Juliet, too, takes her own life.

→

Act 3 Scene 1 is therefore a clear turning point in the drama and helps us to appreciate the theme of fate that is so important to the play, *Romeo and Juliet*:

'Never was a story of more woe,
Than this of Juliet and her Romeo.'

Mark out of 25	Strengths	Weaknesses
Duncan		
Sarah		

Commentary on sample essays on 'Snake' (pages 114–116)

1 Answer A should be ticked. This answer is clearly pre-prepared, and is answering a question in the 2006 paper that read:

> Choose a poem in which there is a noticeable change of mood at one or more than one point in the poem.
>
> Show how the poet conveys the change(s) of mood and discuss the importance of the change(s) to the central idea of the poem.

The opening sentence of the essay begins with key phrases from this 2006 question. Although the candidate has included terms from the correct question in the second sentence of his essay, he then ignores these topics completely and continues to focus on the topic of mood.

2 Answers A and B should both be ticked here. In Answer A, the candidate knows the poem well and supports his comments with appropriate quotations. However, the comments on mood are unrelated to the question he is supposed to be answering. Answer B gives interesting and accurate biographical information that he relates to the topic of the poem, but again this is not the question to be answered!

3 Answer B is most guilty of this. The second paragraph is expressed very fluently, and shows accurate knowledge of the poem, but it fails to mention any of the five topics mentioned in the question. Remember that in a 'closed-list' question like the one from 2007 which the candidates were attempting, you must only choose the topics mentioned. Some questions are 'open-list', where they give one or two examples of literary features and end with an expression like 'or any other feature of your choice'. However, this candidate does not specify any topic, but merely gives a general commentary without any special focus.

4 Answer C should be ticked here. The candidate repeats the key words of the question in her opening sentence. She then explains the main theme of the poem and immediately relates it to the verse form which she goes on to analyse in more detail. In the following two paragraphs she provides analysis of all the topics chosen from the question. This is an acceptable structure, and lends more unity to her essay than if she had decided to look at each topic in turn, which would have been an alternative way of structuring this question. Her comments are all perceptive, accurate and supported by relevant quotations.

Commentary on sample essays on Romeo and Juliet (pages 120–125)

References are to the checklist of features on page 110–111.

The opening paragraph

Duncan's introduction fulfils all the criteria required for an opening paragraph. It identifies an appropriate scene and justifies why it is a turning point. It gives a brief summary of the text. The last sentence gives an indication of how the discussion of the second part of the question will develop.

Sarah's first sentence covers the first three criteria of an opening paragraph accurately. The rest of the paragraph summarises the plot but implies only vaguely that there will be a turning point in that 'it all goes wrong from here'.

The main body of the essay

Duncan explains three valid ways in which the scene is a turning point: the fortunes of the lovers; the structure of the plot, and the mood of the play. These ideas are clearly marked by topic sentences and developed with convincing evidence.

In dealing with the importance of the scene to the overall appreciation of the play, Duncan's essay is strong in this section, also. He provides a clear structure of ideas, which include the importance of the feud, Romeo's character and the forming of the audience's sympathies.

Sarah's essay is largely narrative. Her frequent use of the word 'then' betrays this. She knows the play well, and understands why the scene is a turning point, but her method of showing this is mainly to recount the events. She was on the right lines with her comments on Mercutio's dying words, but the short piece of analysis is swamped by more narrative. She has only a brief and inadequate paragraph on the second strand of the task, with very weak comment, 'you can understand why fights suddenly flare up', which is barely linked to the text.

The conclusion

Duncan's conclusion relates well to the question and shows understanding of the main concerns of the play.

Sarah's conclusion is very thin, and although the theme of fate might have been brought into her essay relevantly, she has not said anything significant about it in the main body of her essay, and so it is unsatisfactory to bring in a fleeting comment at this late stage.

To sum up

Overall, Duncan's essay is better balanced both in terms of how much time he allocates to each strand of the task and the knowledge of the play that he demonstrates. Although Sarah knows the play well, she has not applied her knowledge effectively, spending too much time on retelling the plot at the expense of analysis, and failing to achieve a good balance between the different strands of the task. Her expression is also less fluent and lapses into informality: 'won't'; 'can't stand'. Duncan's quotations clearly illustrate his points of analysis, whereas Sarah's are like pointless decorations.

Glossary

alliteration: repetition of initial and sometimes internal consonant sounds in a phrase

anecdote: a small story, often personal, included to illustrate an idea in a larger piece of work

anticlimax: a sudden falling off at the end of a list that builds up in rank or significance; a sudden relaxation of tension

aside: in drama, words spoken by a character on stage that the audience can hear but other characters cannot, often representing the speaker's thoughts

assonance: repetition of vowel sounds in a phrase

atmosphere: a pervading feeling, caused by features of weather or landscape or built up through imagery or symbolism

character development: in a work of literature, either an actual change in the personality of a character due to various factors or the gradual revelation of aspects of a character

characterisation: the creation and presentation of characters (people) in a text

climax: the culminating point in a list of things that builds in rank or significance; the peak of tension

comedy: play including humorous or joyous events with a happy ending

conflict: mental or physical clash between people of opposing viewpoints

context: the immediate surroundings of a word or phrase; or the precise place in which it is used

contrast: demonstration of differences or opposites in things directly or indirectly compared

denouement: unfolding/explaining of various strands of the plot at the end of a play or novel

dialogue: conversation between two or more characters

emotive: language expressive of strong feeling that stirs emotion in the reader or audience

enjambment: the continuation of a sentence beyond the end of a line or stanza of a poem without a pause

exposition: in drama, providing (usually indirectly) information regarding the background to events through techniques such as dialogue

expression: style of language, including features such as word choice, figures of speech, sentence structure, formal/informal style

features of style: a vague and all-inclusive expression, which can cover word choice, sentence structure, imagery, tone, figures of speech, humour, use of examples etc. (see 'techniques')

figurative language: alternative word for metaphor; contrasts with literal (actual) meaning

figure of speech: general term for language techniques such as simile, metaphor, hyperbole, alliteration, oxymoron, irony, etc.

first person: using 'I', 'we' instead of 'he', 'she', 'they'; the writer appears to be talking to the reader

flashback: a technique of structure where events move back to an earlier time

flashforward: a technique of structure where events move forward to a later time

hyperbole: exaggeration for dramatic or humorous effect

illustration: a detailed example or a small story that acts as an example

image: an unlike thing that something is compared to, which will have one or more points of similarity; for example, in the expression, 'the soldier was as brave as a lion', the image is 'lion', a fearless animal

imagery: a combined term for figurative language in the form of simile, metaphor or personification

irony: saying the opposite of what is really meant for humorous effect; or a twist of fate in events, such as an unexpected coincidence

jargon: technical language or language that is used by specialists of some kind

juxtaposition: placing one thing immediately beside another to create an effect, such as contrast

key incident: an event in the plot of a novel or short story that is important to the development of the whole text in some way

key scene: a scene in a play that is important to the development of the whole drama in some way

monologue: composition put into the mouth of one person, or intended to be spoken by one person

linear structure: placing of events in a story in order of time

link: a sentence (or sentences) that both refers to the idea just discussed and introduces the next one; any joining device in a text; sometimes known as a 'bridge'

metaphor: a comparison where one thing is said to *be* another

metre: regular, rhythmical pattern of stressed/unstressed syllables in verse

mood: a pervading feeling suggested by language or the expression of characters' emotions

narrative technique: method of telling a story, including choice of first or third person, and devices such as diary entries and letters

narrative voice: the persona from whose point of view a literary text is presented

neologism: a new word, or a new meaning for an existing word or expression

novel: a full-length work of prose fiction

onomatopoeia: sound of a word imitates the sense, e.g. sizzle

oxymoron: a phrase containing opposites, e.g. 'frozen fire'

paradox: an apparent contradiction of ideas, e.g. 'you must be cruel to be kind'

persona: a fictitious character who provides the narrative voice in a poem or work of literature

personal: writing that refers to the writer's own experience and feelings, often in the first person; the personality of the writer will be clearly evident (in the case of impersonal writing, the opposite will apply)

personification: an inanimate object is spoken of as if it had a mind of its own

plot: story or scheme of events in a work of literature

register: a form of language used in restricted circumstances; e.g. formal language, medical terminology

rhythm: arrangement or pattern of beats/stresses in verse or language

rhyme: pattern of words whose vowels and final consonants sound the same

second person: using 'you' instead of 'I', 'we', 'they' etc.

sentence structure: how words are arranged in a sentence, and how elements such as subject, verb, object are arranged; repetition, antithesis, listing, climax would all be relevant

setting: where and when the action of a text takes place

short story: complete piece of fiction that is not long enough to be published individually

simile: a comparison using 'like' or 'as'

soliloquy: speech delivered by a character who is alone on stage; usually representing the character's thoughts

sound: in verse, use of techniques such as alliteration, assonance or onomatopoeia that appeal to sense of hearing

stage directions: in drama, instructions on how play is to be performed, including actions, sets, lighting etc.

stage set: scenery and backdrop to action on stage

staging: presentation of a play in performance

stance: point of view

structure: the way a text is put together (e.g. using flashbacks); the development of ideas in a text

style: expression in language

symbolism: indirect representation of ideas through objects, signs or actions; e.g. a flying bird might symbolise escape

synonym: a word that has the same (or similar) meaning as another word

techniques: a broad expression that may include tone, use of illustration, simile, metaphor, alliteration, personification, hyperbole, sentence structure, repetition, listing; use of comparisons, a personal or impersonal approach, etc.

theme: a main idea put across in a text, e.g. the abuse of power

third person: use of 'he'/'she'/'it'/'they', as opposed to 'I'/'we' (first person) or 'you' (second person)

tragedy: a drama involving sad or moving events that ends with the death of one or more main character(s)

tone: the expression of the writer's feelings or attitude to his or her subject

verse form: poetry with regular patterns of lines, rhythm and rhyme; including recognised forms such as sonnet, ode, ballad, etc.

word choice: writer's preference of certain words over others that have similar meanings; also known as diction

Title _____ Genre _____

Author _____

Main characters' names

The Opening _____

_____

_____

_____

The Ending _____

_____

_____

_____

Names of places

Title _____   Author _____

Drama Scene commentary   Act _____   Scene _____

Event	Theme	Characterisation

Title _____   Author _____

Prose commentary   Chapter/episode _____

Event	Theme	Characterisation

Name _____

Class _____   Teacher _____

Date	Assignment
Mark	**Teacher's comment** **My comment**

Date	Assignment
Mark	**Teacher's comment** **My comment**

Date	Assignment
Mark	**Teacher's comment** **My comment**